Grain Sorghum Processing

Health, Ethnic and Industrial Food Products from Grain Sorghum

(*Sorghum bicolour* L. Moench)

U.D. Chavan
Senior Cereal Food Technologist
Sorghum Improvement Project,
Mahatma Phule Krishi Vidyapeeth, Rahuri-413722
Phone: 02426 243670 (R), 02426 243253 (O)
E-mail: uttamch2002@yahoo.co.in

J.V. Patil
Senior Sorghum Breeder
Sorghum Improvement Project,
Mahatma Phule Krishi Vidyapeeth, Rahuri-413722
Phone: 02426 243605 (R), 02426 243249 (O)
E-mail: patiljvp@yahoo.co.in

ibdc publishers

Published by

ibdc publishers

Khushnuma Complex Basement
7, Meerabai Marg (Behind Jawahar Bhawan),
Lucknow 226 001 U.P. (INDIA)
Tel. : 91-522-2209542, 2209543, 2209544, 2209545
Fax : 0522-4045308
E-Mail : ibdco@airtelmail.in

First Edition 2010

Price: Rs. 595/-

ISBN 978-81-8189-471-7

Composed & Designed at :

Panacea Computers
3rd Floor, Agarwal Sabha Bhawan, Subhash Mohal
Sadar Cantt. Lucknow-226 002
Phone : 0522-2483312, 9335927082, 9452295008
E-mail : prasgupt@rediffmail.com

Printed at:

Salasar Imaging Systems
C-7/5, Lawrence Road Industrial Area
Delhi - 110 035
Tel. : 011-27185653, 9810064311

This scientific book is dedicated to our knowledgeable Gurus who taught us a, b, c in the scientific world.

U.D. Chavan
J.V. Patil

Foreword

Sorghum is mostly cultivated in *kharif* and *rabi* seasons in India. Maharashtra ranks first in the production of sorghum grain crop. The production of grain sorghum is higher per hectare in *kharif* season than the *rabi* season. Because during *kharif* season due to occurrence of rain, the water availability is more as well as the climate is warm and humid which is inducive for sorghum growth. Similarly, Agricultural Universities also developed several hybrid genotypes, which yield very high-level grain production.

The *kharif* season sorghum is often vulnerable to rain, gets deteriorated due to mould attack because of the rains mostly occurring during *kharif* season and it makes sorghum grains unfit for human consumption. This ultimately results into the economic loss to farmers.

Such type of problems can be overcome by development of various sorghum-based products. Now-a-days, sorghum is becoming a Nutraceutical crop, because it contains several medicinal properties for curing various types of diseases, mostly diabetes, over weight and so many other disorders. Sorghum consumption is increasing due to its high value in the diet. An up-to-date and scientific information regarding development of various sorghum products, their recipes and nutritive values as well as the procedures for preparation are given in the book on **"Grain Sorghum Processing [Health, Ethnic and Industrial Food Products from Grain Sorghum** ***(Sorghum bicolour*** **L. Moench)]** " written by Dr. U.D. Chavan and Dr. J.V. Patil. I heartily wish them best of luck publication of a book on "sorghum products" which will be beneficial to home product makers (ladies farmers), self-help groups, industrialists as well as students and scientists.

(Dr. R.B. Deshmukh)
Vice-Chancellor
M.P.K.V., Rahuri

Preface

Sorghum is mostly cultivated in *kharif* and *rabi* seasons in India. Maharashtra ranks first in the production of sorghum grain crop. The production of grain sorghum is higher per hectare in *kharif* season than the *rabi* season, because during *kharif* season there is occurrence of rain. So, the water availability is more as well as the climate is warm and humid which is good for sorghum growth. Similarly Agricultural Universities also developed several hybrid genotypes, which yield high-level grain production.

During last decade the *kharif* season sorghum is often vulnerable and the grains gets deteriorated due to mould attack becoming red or black grains because of the occurrence of rains during *kharif* season. During rainy season water accumulation occur in the glumes, which dissolve the pigmented material and spread over all grains. Moist condition supplements various types of fungus growth as well in the grains. Therefore, such type of sorghum grains become unfit for human consumption. This results into the loss of income from sorghum to the farmers.

Such type of problems can be overcome by development of various sorghum-based products. Now-a-days sorghum is becoming a Nutraceutical crop, because it contains several medicinal properties for curing various types of diseases mostly diabetes, over weight and so many other disorders. Sorghum consumption is increasing due to its high value in the diet. The upto date and scientific information regarding development of various sorghum products, their recipes and nutritive values as well as the procedures for preparation are given in the **"Grain Sorghum Processing [Health, Ethnic and Industrial Food Products from grain Sorghum** *(Sorghum bicolour* **L. Moench)]"** book. We hope that this book will be benefited, to the home product makers (ladies), industrialists as well as to the students and scientists.

U.D. Chavan
J.V. Patil

Acknowledgements

Authors are thankful to the Hon. Dr. R.B. Deshmukh, Vice-Chancellor, Mahatma Phule Krishi Vidyapeeth, Rahuri for his critical and fruitful suggestions while the preparation of **"Grain Sorghum Processing [Health, Ethnic and Industrial Food Products from grain Sorghum (*Sorghum bicolour* L. Moench)]** " book. We are thankful to those scientists who worked on development of various value-added products from sorghum and their contribution is acknowledged in this book as well their sources are cited in the reference section. Authors are also thankful to all scientists and friends those helped directly or indirectly while preparation of this manuscript. We would like to express over profound thanks to our family members for their constant support, patience and devotion, which inspired us to complete this manuscript.

U.D. Chavan
J.V. Patil

About the Authors

Dr. U. D. Chavan obtained his B. Sc. and M. Sc. (Agri. in Biochemistry) degrees from Mahatma Phule Krishi Vidyapeeth Rahuri in 1985 and 1987 respectively. He received his Ph.D. degree in Food Science from Memorial University of Newfoundland St. John's Canada in 1999. He has done International training on "Global Nutrition 2002" at Uppsala University Uppsala, Sweden in 2002. He also attended follow-up International workshop on "Global Nutrition 2002" at Hanoi, Vietnam in 2002. Dr. Chavan visited Denmark, Finland, Ireland, France, Switzerland, Poland, Spain, Vietnam, Thailand, England, and U.S.A. under "Global Nutrition 2002" Programme sponsored by Swedish International Development Agency (SIDA). During this programme he worked on human nutritional diet and disorders as well as on genetically modified organisms (GMO).

Dr. Chavan worked as Senior Research Assistant in the Department of Biochemistry and Food Science and Technology at Mahatma Phule Krishi Vidyapeeth Rahuri from 1988 to 2000. During his Ph. D., he worked as Technician/Research Associate at Atlantic Cool Climate Crop Research Center and Agriculture and Agri-Food Canada. He has guided 15 students for M.Sc. (Agri.) in Biochemistry and Food Science and Technology.

Dr. Chavan received Korgavkar Trust Fellowship, undergraduate and post-graduate merit scholarship as well as Senior Research Fellowship from ICAR, New Delhi and United States Department of Agriculture U. S. A. He received University Graduate Fellowship from Memorial University of Newfoundland St. John's Canada for his Ph. D. programme. Dr. Chavan also received International **Scholar Award** and **Excellentiam Award** for his Ph. D. research work from Memorial University of Newfoundland St. John's Canada. He has received a "Certificate of Appreciation" from the U.S. Department of Agriculture in 1992 for his work on processing of groundnut under the guidance of Dr. S. S. Kadam (Principle Investigator). He has written 85 research papers and 40 popular articles. He has authored nine books in Marathi, three books in English and two book chapters in English. He has been awarded "Literary Award" for his best book on "Growth Regular" on agriculture. Dr. Chavan was selected as a best group leader and best presentation for "Global Nutrition 2002" by SIDA. He has been awarded **"Life Time Achievement Award 2004"** for his out standing contribution in post-harvest technology of fruits and vegetables and allied fields by United Writers' Association of India. He has been elected as a Fellow of United Writers' Association of India in 2004. Dr. Chavan received pride of nation and **Maharashtra Gunigan Ratna Award for 2006**. He also received **Jewels of India Award for 2006** for his contribution in the field of Food Science and Technology.

He has given 5 recommendations in the field of Food processing. He also actively involved in the development of NIAW-917 (wheat), SPV-1546, RSV-1626 (Chitra), RSV-423 (Vasudha) and RSV-458 (Annuradha) Sorghum varities. He has given 15 radio talks and 3 TV programmes. Currently he is working as Senior Cereal Food Technologist at Sorghum Improvement Projet, Mahatma Phule Agriculture University, Rahuri.

Dr. J. V. Patil obtained his B. Sc., M. Sc. and Ph. D. degrees (Agri. in Botany, Cytogenetics and plant breeding) from Mahatma Phule Krishi Vidyapeeth Rahuri in 1979, 1981 and 1992 respectively.

Dr. Patil worked on several positions since 1981 as Senior Research Assistant, Jr. Genetist-2, Associate Professor, and Plant breeder, Professor of Botany and now from 2007 he is working as a Head Department of Agricultural Botany and holding additional charge as Sorghum Breeder at Mahatma Phule Krishi Vidyapeeth Rahuri. During his service carrier he worked on several administrative posts in the University. He has guided 12 students for M. Sc. (Agri.) and 5 students for Ph. D. in the discipline of Agricultural Botany.

Dr. Patil received Merit Scholarships during his under and postgraduate study programme. He also received **Baliraja**: Late Annasaheb Shinde Smruti Krishi Sanshodhak Gaurao Puraskar (2004) and **"Vasantrao Naik Krishi Puraskar" (2005)** from Government of Maharashtra. He has written 73 research papers, 48 technical publications and 58 popular articles. He also organized 13 farmers' rallies, and given 27 radio talks and 10 TV programmes. He has developed Girna (safflower), Virat, Vaibhav, Varun, Vipula, Digvijay, Rajas (chickpea), Phule Amruta, Uttara, CSV 19 SS, Chitra, CMS 1409 A/B, RSV 423, (sorghum) crop varieties during his service carrier. He also gave 5 recommendations for farming various crops on farmers field. He also developed several innovative agro techniques such as planting methods, and sprinkler method in irrigated chickpea, technique for in-situe rainwater conservation in *Rabi* sorghum etc.

Contents

Chapter 1

Introduction

Sorghum (*Sorghum bicolour* L. Moench) is one of the major cereal crops among the all millets grown mostly in dryland. It is grown as rainfed crop in both season *Kharif* (monsoon) and *Rabi* (winter). It is mainly grown in the Deccan plateau, Central and Western India apart from a few patches in northern India. Almost entire grain produce is used for human consumption in India. It is nutritionally superior to other fine cereals such as rice and wheat and hence it is known as nutritious cereal. Nutritionally sorghum grain contains 4.4 to 21.1% protein, 2.1 to 7.6% fat, 1.0 to 3.4% crude fibre, 57.0 to 80.6% total carbohydrates, 55.6 to 75.2% starch and 1.3 to 3.5% total minerals (ash). Sorghum also provides 350 Kcal energy, calcium, phosphorus, potassium, carotene and thiamin as well as antioxidants through phenolics and various types of tannins. It is mainly consumed as *Bhkari* (*roti*) i.e. un-leavened pancake in various states of India. Apart from the traditional products like *bhakari, bhatwadi, papad, popped grains, kurdai, high fibre cookies, biscuits, flakes, thalipeeth, upama, rawa idali, dosa, uttappa, chiwada, chakali, papadi, ambil, shankarpale, cookies and cakes* are also prepared from sorghum and consumed as snack food items. Sorghum grains are not only good source of nutrients but it also contains special constituents such as phyto-chemicals, dietary fibre as well as resistant starch, which are more essential to the human nutrition. However, the grain sorghum consumption has remained restricted to the weaker sections of the society due to poor nutritional quality of grain and inferior quality of the products such as Bhakari as well as very low price of this food item as compared to the other cereal grains such as wheat, rice and other millets.

Sorghum is of African origin. A large variety of wild and cultivated sorghum are grown in the tropics and subtropics of the world. In India, sorghum constitutes an important article of food, after rice and wheat. The sorghum grain is small and rounded, varying in colour from off-white to white to varying shades of red, yellow or brown. The grain size varies, the weight ranging from 7.0 to 61 g/1000 grains, with most sorghums weighing 20 – 30 g/1000 grains. The chemical composition of grain sorghum is similar to that of maize. Generally, sorghum has more protein than maize, a lower fat content and about the same amount and proportions of carbohydrate components. The proximate analysis of Indian sorghum grain indicates moisture, 11.9; protein 10.4; fat 1.9; fiber 1.6; carbohydrates 72.6 and minerals 1.6 per cent; minerals present in the grain are calcium, magnesium, potassium and iron.

In comparison with maize, sorghum grain contains approximately the same quantities of riboflavin and pyridoxine but more pantothenic acid, nicotinic acid and biotin. Nicotinic acid occurs in the grain in available form.

Starch is the major carbohydrate of the grain. The other carbohydrates present are simple sugars, cellulose and hemicelluloses. The amylose content of starch varies from 21 to 28%. Starch from waxy varieties contains little amylose. Both waxy and regular starches contain free sugars upto 1.2%. Sucrose being the major constituent (0.85%) followed by glucose (0.09%), fructose (0.09%), maltose and stachyose. Sorghum grain contains no detectable amount of glucoside, but on germination within 3 days old seedling gives 3.5% Dhurin which leads to the poisoning of animals consuming such sorghum seedlings.

The percentage of different protein fractions to the total protein of sorghum grown in India is albumin 5; globulin 6.3; prolamin 46.4 and glutelin 30.4. Prolamin and glutelin are principally present in the endosperm. Amino acid analysis of various protein fractions show that there is better distribution of all essential amino acids in globulins than in prolamins. Sorghum protein is superior to wheat protein in biological value and digestibility. A vegetarian diet based on some varieties of sorghum is somewhat better than a rice-based diet. Sorghum lipids mostly consist of triglycerides, which are rich in the unsaturated fatty acids, oleic and linoleic, their percentage being 33 and 47 respectively.

The nutritional quality of grain sorghum can be improved by malting, fermentation and by mixing of flour from other cereal grains or pulses. Malting or germination of sorghum grain have been reported to improve the nutritional quality in terms of increased soluble proteins, free amino acids, reducing sugars, digestibility of proteins and starch. Such type of grain processing treatments increases dietary fibre content in the final processed products. The higher proportion of dietary fibre of grain sorghum confer many advantages such as nutritional, digestive and physiological benefits such as hypocholesterolemic and hypoglycemic effects, incidence of colon cancer, constipation and gastro-intestinal complications etc. A large number of diabetic patients are regularly consuming sorghum bhakari with fenugreek or bitter gourd *subji* through every day meals. However, the bhakari prepared from malted sorghum flour has been found to contain higher proportion of dietary fibre with superior nutritive and digestive values with additional physiological benefits. Natural sorghum roti consumption has been restricted to only weaker section of the society due to its coarse nature and palatability. This type of problems can be overcome by using malting and fermentation technology for sorghum.

Sorghum is undoubtedly the staple cereal of Botswana and is grown widely in the country. Statistical surveys indicated that 96% population of Southern and Southeastern districts of Botswana mainly consuming sorghum as a major food. Several varieties of sorghum and millet, both indigenous and exotic are grown in the country. All these varieties have proved to be of good food value and may be used for different industrial applications. The development of these varieties and their subsequent use has been steered by a number of institutions in the country and abroad, notably the ministry of Agriculture, SADC/ICRISAT. The Botswana Technology Center (and its international collaborators-CIRAD, NRI and IICT) and others. An identified constraint that continues to higher the national objective of food security is postproduction losses. These losses are believed to be high in magnitude although there are no loss assessment studies carried out in the country. These losses are caused by a number of agents, mainly insects and postproduction practices.

In many parts of the world sorghum has traditionally been used in several food products and various food items, like porridge, unleavened bread, cookies, cakes, couscous and malted beverages are made from this versatile grain. The traditional food preparation of sorghum is quite varied according to the region. Boiled sorghum is one of the simplest uses and small, corneous grains are normally desired for this type of food product. The whole grain may be ground into flour or decorticated before grinding to produce a fine particle product or flour, which is then used in various traditional foods. Sorghum is a good source of lactobacilli, which is used in souring of foods used in traditional fermented foods and drinks. Nigerians produce "*Ogi*" a traditional fermented thin porridge. Fermented breads called "*masa*" and an unleavened bread called "*waina*" are also produced in Nigeria. "*Tuwo*" is a stiff porridge produced in Nigeria by adding boiling water to sorghum flour and continuously stirring. Couscous can be made from sorghum. The grain is also used in making starch, dextrose, syrup, gur, vodka, malted flour for weaning foods, beers, and other alcoholic beverages.

Sorghum play very important role in animal feed production in various countries like the USA, Mexico, South America and Australia. The nutritional value of good quality sorghum has an average feeding value of 96 to 98% of corn. Sorghum can be processed to further improve its food as well as feed value and techniques such as grinding, crushing, steaming, steam flaking, popping and extruding have all been used to enhance the grain for food and feeding purpose. The products are then fed to beef or dairy cattle; egg laying hens, poultry and pigs are also used in pet foods.

Industrial uses for sorghum includes wallboard and biodegradable packaging materials. In addition to the wallboard grain sorghum can be processed interchangeably with corn for the production of ethanol-many ethanol producing factories within the United States use grain sorghum as their principal grain due to their favourable geographic location. A very valuable co-product created from the processing of grain sorghum for ethanol is dry distillers grain. Grain sorghum having high protein animal feed supplement generates additional revenues for the ethanol processing plant.

Benefits of sorghum consumption:

1. Sorghum food provides non-glutinous flours which is useful for avoiding damage to the lining of the intestine and make easy for nutrients to be absorbed
2. It avoid celiac disease problems
3. It helps to prevent dermatitis herpetiforms disease
4. Sorghum is non-acid forming food
5. Sorghum foods are a soothing and easy to digest
6. Sorghum foods are least allergenic and mostly digestible
7. It is good source of dietary fibers
8. It is also good source of vitamins and minerals
9. It also provides antioxidants for controlling cancers
10. Malted sorghum flour can be used for anti-constipation drinks
11. It provides sufficient amount of dietary fiber in human diet
12. Selected sorghum genotypes can provide enough amount of lysine to meet human requirement
13. Sorghum diet is very good to the people suffering from Jaundice
14. Sorghum has very low glycimic index so it helps to human health
15. Sorghum helps in loose and control of body weight
16. It increases body's sensitivity to insulin

17. It also helps in diabetes control
18. It reduces risk of heart diseases
19. It also reduces blood cholesterol levels
20. It also reduces hunger and keeps fuller for longer time
21. It also helps to manage polycystic ovary syndrome in women

Anti nutritional factors and mycotoxins in sorghum:

Sorghum contains polyphenols, which are generally associated with grain pigmentation. Polyphenols commonly referred to as tannins, interfere with the bioavailability of nutrients. It has been reported that sorghum grains contain substantial quantities of condensed tannins and trace amounts of hyrdrolyzale tannins. Brown sorghums with high tannins are known to be resistant to bird depredation and have reduced preharvest germination and grain moulding.

Sorghum grain is known for its hardness compared to other food grains. The hardener of the grain is due to higher content of protein prolamin. Prolamin content varies from 36.0 to 51.0%. The antinutritional factors present in sorghum grain are polyphenols, and phytic acid. Polyphenols are the secondary metabolites produced and the presence of polyphenols/tannins in diet result in poor digestibility of proteins as they bind the proteins present in grain and make them unavailable for the intestinal absorption. Mostly polyphenols present in colored sorghums. In white sorghum, flavan 3-ols or flavan 4-ols (monomers of polyphenols) are present in very low quantity. Apart from flavan 4-ols, phytic acid is also present in sorghum in the form of 6-inositol phosphate. Phytic acid usually forms insoluble compounds with minerals like calcium, iron, magnesium and zinc thus making them unavailable.

Presently the new research investigations on polyphenols and phytic acid consider these compounds as health factors and consumption of these factors increase immunity in animal and human systems against several diseases. Due to grain mould the kharif grain gets severely affected by *Fusarium* and *Aspergillus* fungi, which produce harmful toxins. These mycotoxins namely aflatoxins and fumonisins cause deleterious effects to human and animal health. Hence the grain that is used for food preparation and consumption should be free of these toxins. However these toxins have a safety limit beyond which they cause ill health. The safety limit for aflatoxins is 20 ppb and for fumonisins it is 200 ppb as per the CODEX committee. Aflatoxin contamination was relatively less compared to Fumonisin contamination.

Nutritional enrichment of sorghum with other cereal/pulse grain:

Since the need for nutritive food at low cost is in demand, and majority of the population cannot afford to buy variety of foodgrains for their bread and *roti* preparation, there is a great necessity to make a ready made *atta* with all the possible ingredients in a desired combination. The concept of multigrain flour is more ideal not only for nutritional and cost benefits but to improve the texture and shelf life of the flour. Efforts have been made to make composite flour with sorghum, wheat, maize, ragi, bajra and soybean keeping sorghum up to 50-60%. The kneading quality of the composite flour was very good. Also the roti made of the composite flours was very soft and good in taste. The dough has good viscosity and the mean diameter of the roti made from composite flours was 24.16 cm. as compared to sorghum grain flour, which was 22.39 cm. The composite flour is also ideal for making different foods listed in this book. The composite flour is very useful for children with malnutrition and under nutrition. The composite flour is also ideal to include in the mid day meal programme as the school children need complete balanced diet.

The substitution of sorghum flour to poor vegetarian diets based on sorghum and finger millet increased the protein content of the diet and markedly improved the rate of weight gain in experimental trials. Consumer acceptability tests indicated that groundnut flour could be incorporated up to a level of 20 per cent with sorghum in familiar food preparations. Soybean flour when incorporated in sorghum flour, it was found that the blend of 70 to 30 per cent was found to be the best. This blend had 19 per cent protein and 2.26 PER, which is very close to that of casein (2.5). The blend was used in popular jowar recipes such as *roti* and *laddu,* which were found to be highly acceptable by the people. This blend also satisfied the I.S.I. specifications for infant foods. Therefore, preparations of roti and laddu from sorghum-soybean blend seem to be quite promising in bridging the protein-calorie gap.

Chapter 2

Comparison with other Cereals

2. Comparison with other Cereals

Grain sorghum is mostly used for human food as well as in small quantity for animal feeds. The utilization of sorghum grains in the world is shown in Table 1. From this table it is conformed that most of the sorghum grains are used as food in the Asia and Africa. Developed countries are using very small quantity of sorghum grains as a food and remaining mostly using for animal feeds.

Table 1. Sorghum utilization (average million tones).

Region	Food	Feed	Other uses	Total
Africa	8.0	0.4	2.3	10.7
Asia	15.1	6.3	2.1	23.5
Central America	0.3	8.4	0.2	8.9
South America	-	4.6	0.3	4.9
North America	-	12.6	0.1	12.7
Europe	-	1.4	-	1.4
USSR	-	2.3	0.3	2.6
Oceania	-	0.4	-	0.4
World	**23.4**	**36.4**	**5.3**	**65.1**
Developing countries	23.2	15.6	4.8	43.6
Developed countries	0.2	20.8	0.5	21.5

Sorghum grains are rich in fiber and minerals apart from having a sufficient quantity of carbohydrates, proteins and fat. The comparison of sorghum grain with other cereals is given in following Tables 2, 3, 4, 5, 6 and 7.

Table 2. Average composition of cereal grains.

Grains	Moisture (%)	Crude Protein (%)	True protein (%)	Oil/ Ether extract (%)	Crude fiber (%)	CHO (NFE) (%)	Ash (%)
Barley	15.0	9.0	8.5	1.5	4.5	67.4	2.6
Sorghum	11.0	9.6	8.6	3.8	1.9	71.3	2.4
Maize	13.0	9.9	9.4	4.4	2.2	69.2	1.3
Millet	13.0	10.5	9.9	3.9	8.1	60.7	3.8
Oats	13.0	10.4	9.5	4.8	10.3	58.4	3.1
Rice	11.4	8.3	7.2	1.8	8.8	64.7	5.0
Rice polished	13.0	6.7	6.4	0.4	1.5	77.6	0.8
Rye	13.0	11.6	10.7	1.7	1.9	69.8	2.0
Wheat	13.0	12.2	11.0	1.9	1.9	69.3	1.7

Table 3. Amino acid composition of sorghum, wheat and rice grains (g/16 g Nitrogen).

Amino acid	Sorghum	Wheat	Rice
Lysine	2.60	2.72	3.68
Histidine	2.06	2.08	2.08
Arginine	4.20	4.64	7.68
Aspartic acid	7.21	3.40	4.85
Threonine	3.00	2.88	3.68
Serine	3.66	4.30	4.56
Glutamic acid	20.30	32.50	11.69
Proline	6.25	11.60	5.27
Glycine	3.45	3.20	6.41
Alanine	8.64	2.00	3.23
Cystine	0.97	2.24	1.44
Valine	4.39	4.48	6.08
Methionine	1.39	1.44	2.40
Isoleucine	3.83	3.52	4.80
Leucine	12.27	6.56	8.00
Tyrosine	3.25	2.88	4.64
Phenylalanine	4.55	4.48	4.48
Trptophan	1.12	1.12	1.28
Total	**93.14**	**96.04**	**86.25**
Energy (Kcal)	349	341	345

Table 4. Mineral composition of sorghum, wheat and rice flour (mg/100 g).

Mineral	Sorghum	Wheat	Rice
Sodium	21.00	19.3	2.2
Potassium	537.00	315.0	7.4
Calcium	25.00	48.0	10.0
Phosphorus	526.00	183.0	160.0
Magnesium	212.00	132.0	90.0
Iron	8.48	4.90	0.70
Zinc	3.91	2.20	1.40
Copper	0.86	0.51	0.14
Manganese	3.50	2.29	0.59

Table 5. Vitamins content in sorghum, wheat and rice grains.

Vitamin	Sorghum	Wheat	Rice
β-Carotene (μg/100g)	47.00	64.00	-
Thiamine (mg/100g)	0.37	0.45	0.06
Riboflavin (mg/100g)	0.13	0.17	0.06
Niacin (mg/100g)	3.10	4.30	1.90
Total B6 (mg/100g)	0.21	0.57	-
Folic acid (μg/100g)	20.00	35.80	8.00

Table 6. Oxalic acid, phytic phosphorus and dietary fiber in sorghum, wheat and rice grains.

Constituent	Sorghum	Wheat	Rice
Oxalic acid (mg/100g)	10.00	8.00	3.00
Phytic Phosphorus (mg/100g)	172.00	238.00	83.00
Phytic P as percent of total P	77.00	80.00	52.00
Total dietary fiber (%)	12.69	11.40	-

Table 7. Synergistic effects of legume (green gram) on PER of sorghum.

Source of protein	PER
Casein	2.87
100% Sorghum	0.93
90% Sorghum + 10% green gram	1.11
80% Sorghum + 20% green gram	1.36
70% Sorghum + 30% green gram	1.75
50% Sorghum + 50% green gram	1.56

Chapter 3

Grain Structure and Quality

Many scientists have described the kernel structure of sorghum. The kernel characteristics of sorghum described by using light, fluorescence and electron microscopy. The sorghum kernel can be divided into the following main and sub-components:

A. Seed Coat:

1. Pericarp
    - a. Epicarp
        1. Epidermis
        2. Hypodermis
    - b. Mesocarp
    - c. Cross-cell layer
    - d. Tube-cell layer
2. Testa (not present in all grain types)

B. Embryo or Germ

1. Embryonic axis
2. Scutellum

C. Endosperm

1. Based on hardness (structure)
    - a. Peripheral
    - b. Corneous, vitreous, horny or flinty
    - c. Intermediate
    - d. Floury or soft
2. Based on chemical composition
    - a. Waxy

b. Non-waxy

c. Sugary

Sorghum grain processing involves converting shelled grain into consumable or suitable for further processing. The primary processing events involves cleaning, dehulling (decorticating), pounding and milling into fine powder. Then comes secondary processing, which involves turning raw material into food that includes blending, roasting, fermentation, frying or cooking etc.

Sorghum grain require the removal of the outer layer before any further processing because the milling and sensory qualities of sorghum for *roti / bhakari* making are influenced by the kernel characteristics. More recently, Chavan and Salunkhe (1984) have described the kernel characteristics and their implications in the nutritional and processing properties of sorghum. The sorghum kernel can be divided into seed coat, embryo or germ and endosperm (Plate 1). The seed coat contributes 3 to 10 per cent of dry weight of the kernel. It is made up of four sub-layers: epicarp, mesocarp, cross-cell layers and tube cell layers. The epicarp is subdivided into epidermis and hypodermis. Many times, epidermis contains pigments depending upon the genetic background of the seed. If the kernel is enclosed in pigmented glumes, these pigments migrate to the endosperm, especially, during humid weather or if crop receives rains at late maturity.

The presence of pigments (red, brown, lemon yellow or black) in seed coat or in endosperm posses a serious problem of their separation by pearling or milling which affects the quality of final product. The layer beneath the pericarp is called testa. The testa layer is complete in some sorghum grains, partial, sporadically around the pericarp in some while totally absent in others. These layers contain the polyphenolic pigments called tannins. Due to its fibrous irritating nature and presence of pigments, the seed coat and testa are considered as undesirable parts of the grain from processing and utilization point of view. In the traditional milling process, part of the seed coat and testa are ground to powder, which is not fully separated by shifting the flour through a common sieve leaving considerable amount of bran with tannins in the resultant flour. Therefore, these components need to be effectively removed during milling to improve the quality and acceptability of sorghum products. The embryo or germ contributes to about 8 to 12 per cent of the dry weight of the kernel. It contains oil globules, protein bodies and few starch granules. The germ of some sorghum cultivars is more deeply embedded inside the endosperm and is difficult to remove. The germ contains more proteins that rich in lysine. Hence, a deep placement of embryo is desirable to avoid its loss during pearling or decortications.

The endosperm is the largest component contributing about 81 to 85 per cent to the dry weight of the kernel. It consists of aleurone layer, peripheral (hardest), corneous (hard), intermediate (semi hard) and floury (soft) portions. The aleurone is a single layer of block like rectangular cells and contains a large amount of minerals, water-soluble vitamins, autolytic enzymes, oil, and protein bodies. The remaining portions of the endosperm contain mostly of nutrients such as proteins, starch, oil and minerals of the sorghum grain. The highest protein concentration is in the peripheral region and decreases towards floury area. The major proteins in the outer portions are prolamine, a lysine deficit protein while the proteins in floury region are relatively rich in lysine. The relative proportions of the corneous to floury endosperm within the sorghum kernel (endosperm texture) are known to influence processing properties of sorghum. Usually corneous endosperm is associated with more hardness, less breakage during pearling, easy removal of bran, resistance to pest infestation during storage and higher yields during milling. The physical properties of the grain influence *bhakari* making quality of sorghum. In general, pale yellow grain with intermediate corneous endosperm and with thin pericarp without testa produced *bhakari / roti* with acceptable quality. Waxy and floury grains produce poor quality *bhakari / roti*. The detailed physical properties and chemical composition of various types of grains with typical endosperm character are given in Table 8 and 9. The protein concentration is highest in peripherial endosperm and decrease towards floury. The major protein in the outer portions is prolamin, a lysine deficit protein. This results in the lower concentration of lysine in the peripherial and corneous while the floury endosperm is higher in the lysine content.

Various in the structural features of the sorghum grain are large. Such differences in relative proportions of the seed coat, germ and endosperm structure and types affect the nutritional and processing quality of the grain. Identification of the cultivars early in the breeding programme for specific and uses can be possible by selecting the lines with certain physical characters such as pericarp thickness, presence or absence of testa, endosperm texture, placement and proportion of germ, hardness, and shape of the grain.

The outer layers of certain sorghum varieties seed contain tannins, which are slightly toxic or have a bitter taste. Traditionally the processing of sorghum and millet has been carried out by grinding the whole grain between two plates of stones or by pounding grain using a pestle and mortar. The latter method is the commonest. The grain is then winnowed using leselo to remove the bran. Pounding and winnowing are repeated several times for getting good quality flour. The objective of hand pounding is thus twofold, the first is to remove the bran and the second is to produce the good quality flour, but this is time consuming and backbreaking system.

Table 8. Kernel characteristics, physical properties and proximate analysis of grain sorghum with different endosperm structures.

Parameter	Corneous		Intermediate		Floury	
	Ref: 1	2	1	2	1	2
1000 kernel weight (g)	20.0	19.0 – 28.5	24.0	24.5 – 48.7	22.0	11.6 – 28.8
Hardness, %	33.5	17.9 – 63.8	15.7	1.2 – 44.1	7.2	0.1 – 30.8
Density (g/cm^2)	1.4	1.31 – 1.4	1.37	1.32 – 1.38	1.2	1.22 – 1.36
Protein, %	12.9	13.8 – 17.8	11.8	12.4 – 15.6	16.6	12.6 – 14.6
Lipid, %	2.8	2.8 – 4.1	2.6	3.2 – 4.2	3.4	3.3 – 4.2
Ash, %	1.6	-	1.3	-	1.9	-
Starch, %	73.4	61.5 – 70.5	75.2	68.1 – 71.4	66.7	62.3 – 67.5
Amylose (% in total starch)	29.0	-	29.0	-	28.5	-

Source: 1. Sullins and Rooney, 1974; 2. Karim and Rooney, 1972.

Table 9. Kernel characteristics, physical properties and chemical composition of sorghum grains with different endosperm types.

Parameter	Waxy	Normal	Sugary	Yellow	High-Lysine
1000 kernel weight (g)	27.6 - 34.6	24.5 - 48.7	22.4 - 33.1	26.6 - 59.2	19.3
Hardness, %	4.3 - 43.5	1.2 - 44.1	5.0 - 29.1	16.4 - 29.6	-
Density (g/cm^2)	1.32 - 1.33	1.32 - 1.38	1.29 - 1.30	1.32 - 1.36	-
Protein, %	13.3 - 15.7	12.4 - 15.6	14.7 -17.3	11.4 - 14.0	11.7
Lipid, %	3.4 - 3.7	3.2 - 4.2	5.2 - 5.4	2.7 - 3.7	-
Starch, %	68.8 - 72.6	68.1 - 71.4	60.9 - 64.1	69.7 - 75.9	-
Amylose % (in total starch)	0.79 - 4.8	27.72	26.80	29.82	-
Lysine (g/100g protein)	-	2.34	-	-	3.51

Source: Karim and Rooney, 1972; Miller and Burns, 1970; Sullins *et al.*, 1975.

The improved methods of processing sorghum and millets improve two stages, which use a dehuller and a hammer mill. The dehuller is used to remove the bran from the sorghum before it is milled. A dehuller has an abrasive disc or stones set on a horizontal shaft rotating at a high speed inside a casing. The grinding action of the spinning stones and the friction of the other grains rub off the bran. After primary processing, cereal products, flour or whole grain are further processed in the home and by small cottage industries into final products. Commonly final products from sorghum and millets include foods with porridge, fermented drinks and weaning foods. There is still a great potential for sorghum to be processed into snack foods, breakfast cereals, whole grain foods and baked products.

Chapter **4**

Milling

Dry milling separates the grain into three components, germ, endosperm and seed coat. Milling techniques practiced mostly depend on the end use of the products (Plate 2). Pounding in a mortar and pestle to remove outer bran, with dry or slightly wet grain, does traditional milling (Plate No. 3). After pounding, the outer bran is removed by winnowing and the endosperm is pulverized in the same pestle and mortar or ground as small *chakkai*. Pounding is a very laborious and time-consuming process. Hence the usage of hand pounding is not advantageous to practice in any food enterprise. The dry milling process starts with the cleaning of grains. The cleaned grain is conditioned by addition of water, to soften the endosperm, and milled by the conventional roller mills to separate the endosperm, germ and bran from each other. The endosperm is recovered in the form of grits, with the minimum production of flour. Yields of various fractions from the dry milling process are grit, 76.7; bran 1.2; germ 11 and fiber 10%. Bran and germ are further processed as in the case of maize by dry milling for the preparation of oils and feeds.

A. Milling of sorghum:

Milling process of sorghum is called pearling and decortications. In this case cleaned grains are wetted by spraying water for 2 - 3 min and immediately milled in a rice huller to remove a major part of the coarse fiber, pigment, with minimum degree of cracking of the grain. A maximum of 12% polishing can be carried out. This type of milling can give products rich in protein (upto 27%) and which are also high in fat and give high yield of ash, but are low in fiber. These products are used in the preparation of food products of high protein content.

B. Wet milling of sorghum:

Wet milling of sorghum is carried out by methods similar to that of wet milling of maize. Clean sorghum seeds are steeped for 48 hrs in warm water (50 ^{0}C). Steeping of water softens the kernel and assists separation of the hull, germ and fiber from each other. After steeping, the steep water is drained off, and the sorghum is coarsely ground in degerminating mills to free the germ from the grain. Then the ground material flows down separating through in which hulls and grits settle, while the germ overflows. The degerminated material ground into fine flour.

However, the milling of sorghum is more difficult than that of maize because of the small size and spherical shape of the sorghum kernel and the dense high-protein peripheral endosperm layer. Manufacture of starch is the main purpose of wet milling. However, some of the pigments of the pericarp and sub coat of the grain leach out and stain the starch. Thus grains with dark coloured outer layers are not satisfactory for wet grinding. Sorghum starch is indistinguishable from cornstarch and can be used interchangeably with cornstarch in most industrial applications. Sorghum oil obtained from germ fraction, after refining is used for salads and general cooking. Kernel residues containing bran and gluten are processed as cattle feed.

The starch of waxy sorghums consists almost entirely of amylopectins. These types were developed for starch in the wet milling process. There is some evidence that waxy sorghums may be more digestible. Sticky millet grown in Burma and Hawaii (var. Splendidum) had a more glutinous endosperm and was used to make cakes and sweet meats.

Sorghum can be milled for starch and oil etc. using very similar (wet milling) technology to that of maize. Products were starch (regular or waxy), germ oil and livestock feed. The starch was used in the same way as maize starch, e.g., paper and board, in the food industry etc. Some was converted to sugar, syrup, and dextrin. There were two livestock feeds, gluten feed (21% protein) and gluten meal (41% protein) product.

C. Improved milling methods:

Improved milling methods include roller, milling, pearling, impacting, grinding, and air classification. The roller milled products are reported to have a higher production costs partly due to lower extraction rate. This may not therefore be suitable for adoption of millets commercially. The pearling technique has been applied successfully to sorghum and other millets.

For pearl millet, extraction rates varied between 80 and 90% for similar dehulling times. For elusions only 3 min dehulling is required with extraction rate of 90%. Mechanical dehulling improved physical appearance and functional properties. Dehulling effectively removed the colour of all varieties of sorghum. The detail procedure of mechanical dehulling process is shown in following flow chart (Figure 1, Plate 6). Mechanical dehulling reduces the drudgery. It converts millets into convenient ready-to-cook grain and improves the quality of flour.

Roller milling:

Basically it involves a series of rolls. First, the grooved or corrugated set of rollers break opens the grains. Subsequently, the exposed endosperm is crushed between a series of smooth reduction rollers and freed from the toughened bran. Screening separates the fine grains and the coarse fraction is further fed to the next set of rollers after every pass. The bran is generally, removed by screening and aspiration. The utility of dry milling largely depends upon the maximum yield of endosperm and the use of germ and bran as valuable byproducts. The break flour obtained from the first set of rollers is mostly floury endosperm. It is low in protein, oil, fiber and ash; amounts to 10-15 per cent of the grain; behaves like starch and appears specky. Five fractions of grain sorghum obtained by specific gravity separators (Table 10) and found that the separation of germ more difficult from waxy sorghum than that of non-waxy.

Table 10. Yield and proximate composition of dry-milled non-waxy and waxy (%).

Fraction	Yield	Protein	Oil	Fiber	Ash
Non-Waxy sorghum					
Whole grain	100	9.6	3.4	2.2	1.5
Grits	67	9.6	0.6	0.8	0.5
Bran	12	8.9	5.5	8.6	2.4
Germ	11	15.1	20.0	2.6	8.2
Fines	10	7.1	2.4	1.3	1.0
Waxy sorghum					
Whole grain	100	9.8	3.2	2.2	1.6
Grits	65	9.8	1.0	0.8	0.6
Bran	15	7.1	4.8	11.3	2.1
Germ	14	15.3	18.7	3.0	8.5
Fines	6	6.5	2.3	1.5	1.0

Attrition milling

The attrition mill fitted with saw-tooth blade plates, which provide the dehulling/pearling action (Plate No.4). The grains were further abrased by a drum rotating in a cylindrical screen. Finally, the hulls were separated from the kernels by an air separator. Most attrition type dehullers comprise two stone or metal discs, either or both of them rotate around a vertical or horizontal axis. The attrition is provided by introducing metal pins or blades into the surface of either or both of the rotors or the rotor and stator.

Abrasive milling

The abrasive mill consists of 13 carborundum stones (12-inch diameter), which can be driven at a speed up to 200 rpm (Plate No. 5). In continuous operation, grains are fed through a hopper at one end and released after stone action through an overflow outlet at the other end. The amount of kernel removed as fine is determined by the retention time in the mill, which in turn, depends upon the grain-feeding rate. After discharge from the mill the grain was passed through the air separator on the attrition mill to remove the fines. In addition to efficiency, other factors such as size, maintenance requirements and convenience favour the use of abrasive over attrition type mill for a village scale milling operation.

Sorghum Semolina

Improvement in primary process itself has helped in getting fine sorghum flour. Use of appropriate milling procedures and sieves help in getting sorghum semolina. Fine quality sorghum flour can be substituted in place of Bengal gram flour and wheat flour or wheat semolina. The process developed for sorghum flour and semolina is shown in Figure 2. In a similar manner, pearl millet, ragi and maize flour and semolina can be obtained.

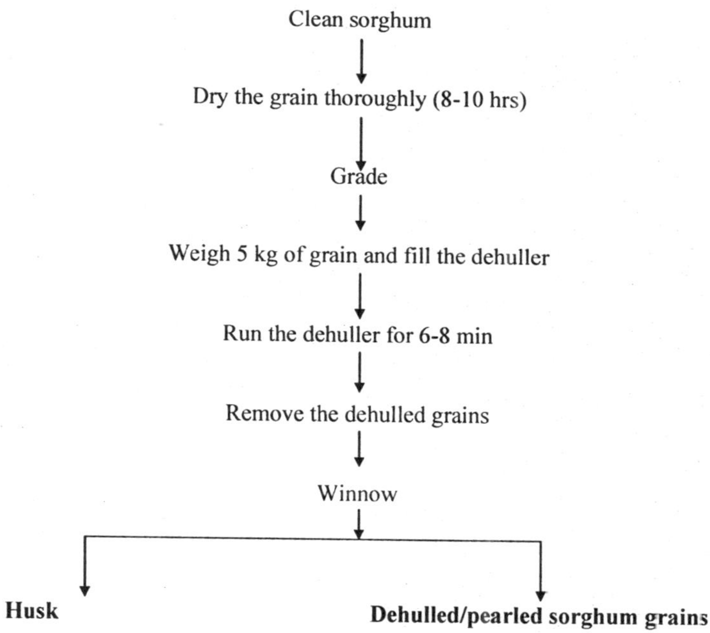

Figure 1. Mechanical dehulling of sorghum grains

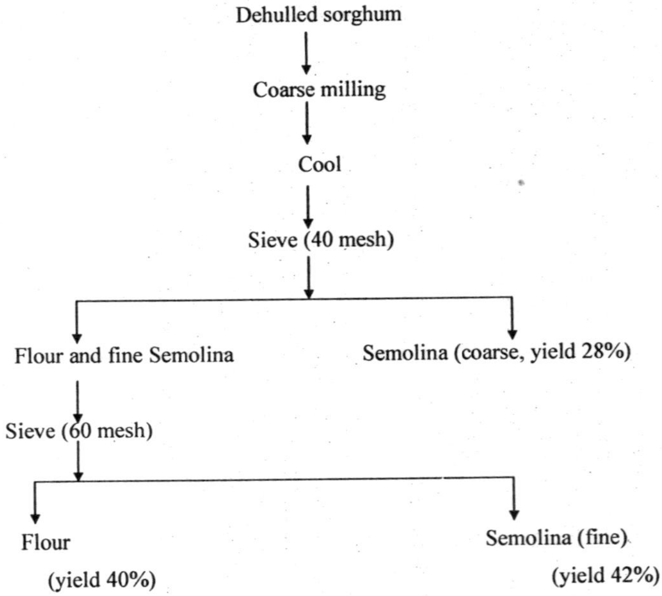

Figure 2. Processing of dehulled sorghum in to semolina.

Chapter 5

Sorghum Protein Digestibility

The human feeding trials results underlined the need for a better understanding of sorghum food preparation so that the protein present in the grain may be made fully available in the food prepared from it. Cooked maize and millet showed protein digestibilties of 82 - 87 per cent, but that for ordinary sorghum was only 56 per cent. However, high-lysine sorghum (P721-Q) gave the better level of 73 per cent protein digestibility. This difference in these two types of sorghum genotype may be due to the prolamin proteins were the main source of protein indigestibility in normal sorghums, and they suspected that the problem lay in the formation of protein polymers linked by disulphide bonds. By cooking normal sorghum in the presence of an appropriate reducing agent, protein digestibility increased to 25 per cent, whereas there was no improvement in barley, rice or wheat when cooked in this way. Reducing agents found suitable included 2-mercaptoethanol, dithiothreitol, sodium bisulphate, and L-cysteine.

Chapter 6

Fermentation

Pre-fermentation processing of cereals:

Pre-fermentation processing of cereals is largely dependent on the end product desired. In most cases, grains are sun dried prior to fermentation. Treatments such as washing, steeping, milling and sieving are pre-fermentation processing steps applied in the cereals.

Fermented cereals:

Plant tissues or animal tissues subjected to the action of microorganisms and or enzymes to give desired biochemical changes and significant modification of food quality are referred to as fermented foods. Fermentation is the oldest known form of food biotechnology; records of barley conversion to beer date back than 5000 years. According to Steinkraus the traditional fermentation of foods serves several functions.

1. Enrichment of the diet through development of a diversity of flavours, aromas and textures in food substrates.
2. Preservation of substantial amounts of food through lactic acid, alcoholic, acetic acid, and alkaline fermentations.
3. Enrichment of food substrates biologically with protein, essential amino acid, essential fatty acids, and vitamins.
4. Detoxification during food fermentation processing.
5. A decrease in cooking times and fuel requirements.
6. Easily digestible and available quickly to the body.

Aside from alcoholic fermentations and the production of yogurt and leavened bread, food fermentations continue to be important primarily in developing countries where the lack of resources limits the use of techniques such as vitamin enrichment of foods, and the use of energy and capital-intensive processes for food preservation. The technology of producing many indigenous fermented foods from cereals remains a household art in these countries. Prospects for applying advanced technologies to indigenous fermented foods and for the production of value added additive products such as colours; flavours, enzymes, antimicrobials and health products during food fermentations have been well reviewed by cook.

Chapter **7**

Indigenous Fermented Cereal Foods

Mot bacterial fermentations produce lactic acids; while yeast fermentation results in alcohol production. Many of the indigenous fermentation products of cereals are valued for the taste and aroma active components produced and are used as seasonings and condiments. A summary of flavour compounds formed in such fermented products is complied by Chavan and Kadam (1989). A number of fermented products utilize cereals in combination with legumes, thus improving the overall protein quality of the fermented product. Cereals are deficit in lysine, but are rich in cystine and methionine. Legumes on the other hand are rich in lysine but deficit in sulphur containing amino acids. Thus by combining cereals with legumes the overall protein quality is improved. The Chinese concept of "*fan*" (rice) and "*tsai*" (other vegetables) for a balanced and interesting diet is seen throughout the world.

Chapter 8

Importance and Advantages / Benefits of Fermented Cereals

Fermented foods contribute to about one-third of the diet worldwide. Cereals are particularly important substrates for fermented foods in all parts of the world and are staples in the Indian subcontinent, in Asia and in Africa. Fermentation causes changes in food quality indices including texture, flavour, appearance, nutrition and safety. The advantage of fermentation may induce improvement in palatability and acceptability by developing improved flavours and textures; preservation through formation of acidulants, alcohol and antibacterial compounds; enrichment of nutritive content by microbial synthesis of essential nutrients and improving digestibility of protein and carbohydrates; removal of antinutrients, natural toxicants and mycotoxins; and decreased cooking times.

Natural fermentation of cereals increases their relative nutritive value and available lysine. Bacterial fermentations involving proteolytic activity are expected to increase the biological availability of essential amino acids more than yeast fermentation, which mainly degrade carbohydrates. Starch and fiber tend to decrease during fermentation of cereals. Although, it would not be expected that fermentation would alter the mineral content of the product, the hydrolysis of chelating agents such as phytic acid during fermentation, improves the bioavailability of minerals. Changes in the vitamin content of cereals with fermentation vary according to the fermentation process, and the raw material used in the fermentation. B group vitamins generally show an increase on fermentation. Fermentation of corn meal and soybean-corn meal blend lowers flatus producing carbohydrates, trypsin inhibitor and phytates.

However, fermentation of cereals with fungi, such as *Rhizopus oligosporus* has been reported to release bound trypsin inhibitor, thus increasing its activity. Fungal and lactic acid fermentations have also been reported to reduce aflatoxin B1; sometimes by opening of the lactone ring which results in complete detoxification.

Chapter 9

Fermented Foods

A. Ambil:

Ingredients	Quantity
Sorghum flour	1000 g
Curd	500 g
Salt	To taste
Water	As per requirement

Ambil is a Maharashtra's popular fermented beverage. For the preparation of ambil the sorghum flour slurry is mixed with curd, salt and fermented overnight and then heat for 5 – 10 minutes, cooled and it is mixed in various proportion with species of condiments and used as beverage during meals.

B. Injera:

Injera is the most popular baked product in Ethiopia. It is fermented sorghum bread with a very sour taste and is the undisputed national bread of Ethiopia. The baked product is referred to by different names depending on the locality of production in Ethiopia. It is referred to as 'bidena' in Oromigua, "taeta" in Giragiua, and "solo" in Walaytigna. According to a report by Gebrekidan and Gebrettiwat over 8% of total sorghum production in Ethiopia is used for 'Injera' production. The sorghum grains are dehulled manually or mechanically and milled to flour, which is subsequently used in the preparation of injera. The flow diagram for preparation of injera is given in Figure 3 and various sources of flour are used for preparation and their nutrient content is given in Table 11.

On the basis of production procedures three types of injera are prepared.

1. **Thin injera:** This type of injera can be prepared from mix-

ing a portion of fermented sorghum paste with three parts of water and boiling to yield a product known as 'abist' which is in turn mixed with a portion of the original fermented flour.

2. **Thick injera:** This type of injera is reddish in colour with a sweet taste, is a 'tef' paste that has undergone only minimal fermentation for 12 – 24 hrs.
3. **Komtata type injera:** This type of injera is produced from over-fermented paste and has a sour taste. The paste is baked or grilled to give a bread-like product. Yeasts are the major microorganisms involved in the fermentation of the sweet type of injera.

Sorghum flour

↓

Mix with water (4:1, w/v)

↓

Knead to form dough

↓

Mix with starter

(Fermented yellowish liquid saved from previous fermented dough)

↓

Knead

↓

Add water

↓

Ferment for 48 hrs

↓

Add water and allow standing for 1 hr

↓

Bake on hot greased clay griddle mental till holes begin to form on top

↓

Injera

Figure 3. Flow diagram for the preparation of injera.

Table 11. Nutritional composition of injera prepared from different cereals (per 100g).

Nutrient	Sorghum	Corn	Finger millet	Barley	Wheat	Tef
Energy (Kcal)	193	185	172	167	172	162
Moisture, %	52.0	54.0	56.1	58.0	57.4	59.8
Protein, %	7.1	5.0	3.8	3.5	5.4	4.2
Fat, %	0.6	0.7	0.3	0.3	0.9	0.6
Carbohydrates, %	39.8	39.6	38.4	37.5	35.6	33.6
Fiber, %	0.9	0.7	4.0	0.9	0.9	1.7
Ash, %	0.5	0.7	1.4	0.7	0.7	1.5
Calcium, mg	10	27	169	16	28	64
Phosphorus, mg	111	120	103	128	155	129
Iron, mg	3.5	2.1	17.3	4.2	3.3	30.5
β-Carotene, μg	0	Trace	Trace	0	0	0
Thiamin, mg	0.17	0.14	0.14	0.12	0.14	0.21
Riboflavin, mg	0.08	0.06	0.01	0.05	0.09	0.07
Niacin, mg	1.7	0.7	0.2	3.0	2.4	0.8
Ascorbic acid, mg	0	2	1	0	1	1

C. Kisra:

This is a thin pancake like leavened bread prepared from whole sorghum flour. It is a dietary staple food in Sudan. This fermented sorghum bread has a very sour taste. It is prepared by mixing sorghum flour with water to give a thick paste which is allowed too ferment for 12-24 hrs, following which the paste is thinned to a desirable consistency with chalked pericarp and without a sub coat gives the best sensory properties. El-Tinay reported that there was a slight increase in protein and fiber and an appreciable decrease in carbohydrate (starch and sugars) during the fermentation of Kisra. An amino acid analysis of Kisra indicated slight differences in the levels of the various amino acids. The detail procedure for preparation of Kisra is given the following flow chart (Figure 4).

Sorghum flour

↓

Mix with water (60:40 w/v)

↓

Ferment for 12-24 hrs

↓

Add water to form thin slurry

↓

Bake on hot oiled pan

↓

Kisra

Figure 4. Flow diagram for the preparation of Kisra.

D. Bogobe:

Bogobe is a sorghum porridge prepared in Botswana from fermented and non-fermented sorghum (Figure 5). Fermented bogobe is a soft porridge, known as ting while the non-

Sorghum grains

↓

Wash with water

↓

Dehull (mechanical or manual)

↓

Discard bran and grind to a coarse meal

↓

Add lukewarm water (1:1 w/v) to form slurry

↓

Allow fermenting in a closed environment for 24 hrs

↓

Cook in boiling water for 12 – 15 min

↓

Bogobe

Figure 5. Flow diagram for the preparation of bogobe from sorghum.

fermented bogobe is a thick porridge called monokwane. Information relevant to the microorganisms involved in the fermentation of bogobe and the nutritional changes, which occur during fermentation, is still scanty.

E. Ogi:

Ogi is a porridge prepared from fermented sorghum, maize, or millet in West Africa. It is a staple of that region, and serves as a weaning food for infants. The traditional preparation of ogi involves soaking of corn kernels in water for 1 to 3 days followed by wet milling and sieving to remove bran, hull and germ. The pomace is retained on the sieve and later discarded as animal feed while the filtrate is fermented for 2 – 3 days to yield ogi, which is sour, white starchy sediment. Ogi is often marketed as a wet cake wrapped in leaves or transparent polythene bags. It is diluted to a solid content of 8 to 10% and boiled into a pap or cooked and turned into a stiff gel called "agidi" or "eko" prior to consumption.

Nutritional and microbiological studies showed that the lactic acid bacterium *Lactobacillus plantarum*, the aerobic bacteria *Corynebacterium* and *Aerobacter*, the yeasts *Candida mycoderma, Saccharomyces cerevisiae* and *Rhodo torula* and molds *Cephalosporium, Fusarium, Aspergillus* and *Penicillium* are the major organisms responsible for the fermentation and nutritional improvement of ogi. *Lactobacillus plantarum* was the predominant organism in the fermentation responsible for lactic acid production. *Corynebacterium* hydrolysed cornstarch to organic acids while *Saccharomyces cerevisiae* and *Candida mycoderma* contributed to flavour development.

Steeping, milling and sieving are the processing steps during which considerable nutrient losses take place. Much of the protein in cereal grains is located in the testa and germ, which are usually sifted off during processing. A protein enriched ogi containing 10% soybeans flour was developed by the Federal Institute of Industrial Research Oshodi (FIIRO) Lagos, Nigeria. The development of an ogi product (*dogik*) having therapeutic properties on the basis of its ability to control diarrhoea among infants. This finding is of great relevance since ogi is used as a popular weaning food for children in African countries. Odunfa *et al.* (1994) investigated the possibility of improving the limiting lysine level in ogi. Fifty mutants from *Lactobacillus plantarum* and seven mutants from yeast strain were selected from thialysine-resistant cultures capable of overproducing lysine and analyzed for lysine production. Up to 12 fold increase in lysine production was observed from *Lactobacillus plantarum* and 3 - 4 fold increase from yeasts was observed. Utilization of the mutants as starter cultures resulted in a three-fold increase in the lysine content of ogi. The use of high lysine corn for improving the nutritional value of ogi is the best way. Dehydration of ogi by drum or tray drying has been shown to prolong its shelf life. Drum drying was however reported to destroy heat sensitive nutrients in ogi. Some scientist reported that an appreciable loss in the available lysine content of ogi as a result of drum drying. Bacteriocin-producing *Lactobacillus* isolated to be active against common food-borne pathogens including *Salmonella*. This bacteriocin also improved the shelf life of "jellied" ogi extending it by 10 days.

F. Masa

This is fermented bread made in Nigeria. A similar batter is used, though thicker in consistency and mixed with onion, pepper, and salt before fermentation. It is fried in oil on both sides as small individual hemispheres.

G. Gahlet

It is a small thick leavened cakes made in Burkina Faso. The weaning food, nasha is made from the same kind of flour and water mixture as Kisra, but is allowed to ferment for 2 days or longer. It is then added to about half the volume of boiling water, and cooked until it thickens.

H. Quitta

This is unleavened bread used to only a small extent in Ethiopia.

I. Waina

This is unleavened bread made in Nigeria; it contains hot pepper and spices, and a substantial amount of groundnut oil. These ingredients are mixed to form dough, which is cut into flat discus and fried in oil.

J. Stiff porridges

The stiff porridge is made by adding flour steadily to boiling water, stirring all the time to avoid lumps, then cooking. The product should be stiff enough to mould without cracks, it should be neither sticky nor crumbly. Names of porridges according to country and region; *Ugali* in East Africa, *Genfo* in Ethiopia, *Guma* in Sudan, and *Tuwo* in Nigeria.

K. Tortillas

The sorghum grains are cooked in limewater in the first stage in Latin America. Prepare mesa by mixing lime solution (0.5 per cent) and sorghum grain in 3:1 proportion and cooking for 3 to 10 minutes at the boiling point. Steep sorghum grains for at least 4 hours. Prepare balls from the mesa and press them into circles of about 15 cm diameter and 0.5 cm thickness. Cook the tortillas on a grill or a traditional clay comale. During cooking turn the tortilla once to brown it lightly on both sides. Leave the cooked tortillas on the floor to cool a little, and then keep them in a container lined with a cloth to cover.

L. Couscous

This type of product is mostly prepared in West Africa. Wet the finely ground sorghum flour with cold water and knead it until flour particles agglomerate. Force the mixture through a fine screen (1.5 mm mesh). Place the grains in a perforated pot fitted over another pot containing boiling water. Put a cloth seal at the joint between the two pots. Heat the lower pot to steam the grains above for about 15 minutes. They will form a single large chunk. Take out the chunk, break it into small aggregates and transfer them back to steam for another 15 minutes. Remove the chunk, break it into aggregates and sift them through a sieve (2.5 mm, mesh). Dry and store for future use. To prepare couscous for serving, sprinkle cool water on the aggregates. Mix thoroughly with fingers. Mix the grains with ground baobab leaf powder or okra powder and other ingredients such as peanut paste, etc. and give it a final steaming for 15 minutes. Allow it to cool slowly. Serve with sauce or milk, or dry it and use as a convenience food.

M. Fura

Fura product is mostly prepared from sorghum and used as a main food in Nigeria.

Ingredients	Quantity
Sorghum flour	200 g
Hot spices	2 tea spoons
Yoghurt or sour milk	100 ml
Water	300 ml approximately

First mix flour, water and spices together. Prepare small round balls (2-3 cm in diameter). Drop them into boiling water and cook for 30 minutes. Pound cooked balls with water and spices until a smooth, elastic and cohesive lump is formed. Again prepare small balls; rolling between the palms of the hand or on a wooden board dusted with dry flour. Serve as it is or with nono, yoghurt or sour milk, as a snack.

Chapter 10

Sorghum Beer

In several African countries sorghum malt is fermented into beer. The beer making process may depend upon local practices and types of cultivars used. Use of sorghum as a brewing grain is gaining popularity not only in other countries of African but also places like Mexico due to rising import cost of barley malt. Some researchers carried out trials on use of sorghum malt in making layer beer in Botswana. A three stage decoction system of mashing was used and the product was acceptable by the consumers. A popular process is being used for making Nigerian sorghum beer in a traditional way. European types of beers were investigated by studying bottom fermentation brewing with Nigerian sorghum malt, sorghum barley beers scored identically. Recently pilot experiment was done successfully for processing sorghum malt to produce lager beer using Nigerian sorghum. In recent year some scientists in India prepared pure sorghum and sorghum-barley malt based beer, which were acceptable to the consumer panel. Ogundiwin and Tehinse conducted fermentation test on malted sorghum wort in the traditional Nigerian pito drink. Effect of adding enzymes to a mixture of malt and sorghum during brewing process on taste, foam stability and chill sensitivity qualities of beer was studied and it was observed that there was increase in soluble carbohydrate and nitrogen, decrease in wort viscosity, higher filtration rate and increased yield. The sorghum grain is without husk unlike barley and hence it causes wort filtration problems.

Karif beer has always good acceptance and acts as a source of B vitamins to Banu people. It has been reported that beer has calorific value of 400 – 500 Kcal/Lit and thiamin 1 –2 mg/lit, Novellie (1977) reported high vitamin contents of sorghum beer.

Heerden analyzed commercially brewed sorghum beer for thiamin, riboflavin, nicotinic acid and protein and reported that sorghum beer had higher thiamin, riboflavin and mineral content than barley beers. Whole sorghum beers were more nutritive than sorghum beer with maize grits as adjuncts. A new sorghum beer product, known as "Long life" is being produced in South Africa, pasteurized and aseptically packaged in tetra pack. Okrafor and Aniche have developed a hop substitute for sorghum beer using a West African herb *Gongronema lactifolium* locally known as "Utazi".

Merissa beer is prepared from sorghum. The sorghum grains are soaked, malted for 2 days and milled to coarse grain. Ajeen, fermented dough is obtained by mixing sorghum flour with water and incubating for 36 hrs. The ajeen is cooked in hollow steel containing until it turns dark brown (soorji). The soorji is then mixed with 5% malt flour, 5% good Merissa and water and allowed to ferment for 4 to 5 days (deboba). A cooked sorghum paste, futtara, is obtained by mixing cooked greenish yellow and brown pastes. Malt flour is mixed with the futtara and placed underneath the doboba surface as a solid mass. Fermentation and liquefication proceed for 8 to 10 hrs. The mass is strained to yield merissa. The principal microorganisms in Merissa fermentation are lactic acid bacteria and *Saccharomyces spp.* of yeast. The detail procedure is given in Figure 6.

Conversion time is the saccharification rate during mashing process. Shorter the conversion time better is the brewing quality of the malt. CSH - 9 and HES - 4 required 7 - 10 min of conversion time and this is considered good. SPV 297 and M 35 -1 required conversion time 10 - 15 min, which is also in acceptable range. The specific gravity of sorghum malt extracts was slightly lower as compared to the literature values for barley malt extracts. The specific gravity of wort from HFS - 4 and M 35 -1 was comparable. HES - 4 and M 35 -1 had higher extract yields as compared to the other two cultivars. Iodine reaction of all wort samples was yellowish indicating absence of starch in the wort and hence sorghum worts were comparable. Colour of the wort from sorghum malt was darker as compared to barley wort. Wort viscosity of M 35 – 1 was slightly higher as compared to the wort viscosity of other cultivars. However, the viscosity of sorghum wort was comparable to barley wort (Table 12).

Total nitrogen content of beer wort of HES – 4 was higher as compared to the values for other three sorghum cultivars. However, mean total nitrogen content to the values for other three sorghum cultivars was comparable to the total nitrogen content of barley wort. Free amino nitrogen (FAN) content of sorghum worts was slightly lower as compared to the barley wort but the varietal differences were also observed. The extract of FAN formation is a function of proteolytic activity in the malt as well as action of carboxy peptidase action during mashing at lower temperature. A balance must be struck between breakdown of proteins to amino acids for yeast nutrition and preservation of high molecular weight proteins, which enhance the foaming properties of the beer. Excessive proteolytic activity may cause hydrolysis of high degree of the large molecular weight.

Neutral polypeptides result into poor foaming and head retention in beer. The third condition with respect to the removal of proteins combine with polyphenols from acid protein fraction in beer, which contributes to haze formation in beer, hence its early removal enhances the stability of beer. Hence removal of basic proteins in wort is essential. However, if the basic protein is insoluble by fixing to the spent grains, it may act as a wort clarifier and remove trouble some polyphenols from the wort.

Total sugars and reducing sugars of the sorghum wort and barley wort were comparable. The varietal differences were negligible for sugars. The values of total sugars and reducing sugars were comparable to those reported by earlier workers. Some scientists reported that lower reducing sugars in wort and hence they used 30 per cent sucrose as adjunct in the wort prior to fermentation. Several studies have been conducted on barley malt mashing and the resultant fermentable sugar content due to enzymatic degradation of starch during mashing has been considered as the most important biochemical reaction.

Acidity and pH of sorghum wort was comparable to that of barley wort and this value is in acceptable range required for the beer fermentation.

After the wort is cooled it is pitched with required quantity of yeast and then immediately the fermentation begins. The first sign of fermentation is the production of gas bubbles, which collects as forth. The fermentation is normally completed in 7 days. The growth of the yeast in fermenting wort causes several biochemical changes particularly it respect to specific gravity, extract content, pH and sugars which are reduced in quantity, whereas there is increase in alcohol production. There is significant reduction in specific gravity of wort during beer fermentation and the reduction is proportionate to the time of fermentation. The differences in the rate of specific gravity reduction were negligible due to cultivars in sorghum wort. There was reduction in extract content of the wort and the rate of change of extract content was similar to that of reduction in specific gravity. The reduction in extract content was from 9.24% to 2.52% in 7 days of fermentation of wort from HES - 4 sorghum. During 7 days of fermentation the wort pH was reduced in all the samples. The change was proportionate for all the sorghum cultivars and comparable to barley wort.

Reducing sugar was found to be reducing proportionately and at almost constant rate as fermentation proceeded. A slight variation in reduction was observed due to cultivar but overall the rate of and the extent of reduction in reducing sugar constant of sorghum wort was comparable to barley wort. The yeast utilized sugars to produce alcohol as the end product. The rate of reducing sugar utilization by yeast was high during first 5 days of fermentation. The rate of utilization of reducing sugar decreased thereafter.

The formation of alcohol during the fermentation of beer wort is a function of yeast growth. The rate of increase in alcohol content was proportional to the yeast growth and consumption of sugars. The rate of alcohol production was constant upto 5 days and then it decreased slightly. Sorghum varietal differences in the rate of alcohol production during fermentation were very negligible and were comparable to barley wort fermentation. The choice of yeast, the condition of yeast at the time of pitching, the amount of yeast added, the distribution of yeast and type of fermenting vessel, aeration, wort composition and pH, fermentation temperature are some of the main factors influencing fermentation performance and beer quality.

Specific gravity of beer from sorghum cultivars ranged from 1.0092 to 1.00985. The apparent extract of sorghum beer was not affected by cultivar and was comparable. Real extract content of beer from CSH - 9 was higher than beer of HES - 4 and M 35 -1 but it was comparable with control barley beer (Table 13). Attenuation is the degree of fermentation in beer based on loss in the specific gravity of the wort. Apparent attenuation of sorghum beers was comparable for all the four cultivars. However, sorghum beer had slightly higher apparent degree of fermentation as compared to control barley. The variation in samples for attenuation could be attributed to basic differences in wort composition with respect to available nutrients for the growth of the yeast. Real attenuation for CSH - 9 and SPV - 297 were comparable with barley beer whereas M 35 - 1 and HES - 4 had higher per cent real attenuation. A high attenuation is the result to wort composition. Attenuation limit can be increased by addition of external enzyme sources.

The scores obtained from various sensory characters like colour, clarity, body, aroma, taste and overall acceptability were statistically compared after transmission of sources to square roots. Colour of the beer prepared from HES - 4 and M 35 -1 sorghum malt was significantly superior over control barley malt beer as well as beer prepared from other sorghum cultivars. However, commercial beer sample had significantly superior beer colour. The colour of the beer is largely due to the melanoidins and caramel present in the malt and adjuncts used. Further caramelization can occur during wort boiling and major adjustments to the colour of beer can be made by the addition of caramel. Hence varietal impact on beer colour is of very little value in the control of beer quality (Table 14).

Body of beer refers to fullness given by the beer sip in the mouth. Perhaps this is related to beer viscosity as felt in the mouth. The body of the beer sample of M 35 – 1 was comparable with commercial beer sample. All the experimental beer samples had acceptable beer aroma. The principle higher alcohols found in beer are 3-methyl butanol, 2-methyl butanol, propanol and phenethyl alcohol, which are responsible for beer aroma. Sensory evaluation of taste of experimental beer samples indicated that all the samples were in acceptable range. From all these experimental information it can be concluded that sorghum can be very well used for the production of beer.

Sorghum grains

↓

Soaking

↓

Germination

↓

Malt is dried

↓

Ground to fine flour (malt flour)

↓

Malted flour

↓

Add cold water to prepare slurry

↓

Add more pounded/steeped sorghum grains in it

↓

Keep for fermentation (required period)

↓

Beer

Figure 6. Preparation of sorghum beer.

Enzymes in the malt begin to saccharify the starch. Bacteria then act on a part of the sugar to form lactic acid and some B vitamins. This sweet wort may be drunk after less than one-day fermentation. It contains more B vitamins and negligible amount alcohol. After the first day, the mixture is heated and various fungal spores germinate and lead to the production of hydrolytic enzymes. A little millet or sorghum may be specially germinated, then dried as a yeast source. The yeasts multiply and fermentation develops, with the production of alcohol, more B vitamins, and new proteins, while the bacteria continue to develop lactic acid. The brew may be drunk after 4 – 5 days, and in some areas more malted grain may be added to it a day before it is used.

Table 12. Properties of sorghum malt for brewing

Genotype	Conversion time, min.	Speed of filtration	Degree of clarity	Colour of malt EBC units
CSH – 9	7 - 10	Slow	Slightly hazy	1.85
SPV – 297	10 – 15	Slow	Slightly hazy	1.60
M 35 – 1	10 – 15	Slow	Clear	1.55
HES – 4	7 – 10	Slow	Clear	1.80

Table 13. Comparative evaluation of worts from sorghum and barley malt.

Genotype	SP. gravity	Original extract optical density	Iodine reaction	Colour EBC units	Viscosity Cp
CSH – 9	1.03360	8.444	Yellowish	9.20	2.42
SPV – 297	1.03435	8.620	Yellowish	9.00	2.61
M 35 – 1	1.03602	9.060	Yellowish	8.00	2.85
HES – 4	1.03690	9.240	Yellowish	9.40	2.35
Barley	1.04160	10.380	Yellowish	7.30	2.45

Table 14. Sensory evaluation of sorghum beer as affected by cultivars*.

Genotype	Colour	Clarity	Body	Aroma	Taste	Overall acceptability
CSH – 9	2.64	2.51	2.55	2.53	2.56	2.66
SPV – 297	2.65	2.51	2.60	2.64	2.60	2.69
M 35 –1	2.67	2.43	2.77	2.74	2.65	2.76
HES – 4	2.75	2.52	2.76	2.72	2.61	2.74
Barley	2.59	2.75	2.87	2.84	2.75	2.84
Commercial	2.82	2.98	2.80	2.97	2.94	2.94
S.E. ±	0.032	0.031	0.025	0.024	0.022	0.021
CD at 5%	0.089	0.087	0.070	0.067	0.061	0.060

*Values are means of square root transformed scores.

Chapter 11

Bhakari / Roti (Unleavened Bread)

This is unleavened bread widely used in India. Whole sorghum is finely ground, a little salt is added, and it is mixed with hot water little by little to make separate balls of dough. These are pressed by hand into flat discs, and baked on both sides in a shallow pan. Cooking time depends upon the thickness of the disc. *Roti* should remain soft a full day and there are genotypic differences in this character.

Dough quality: Flour that can give good, cohesive dough generally produces an acceptable *roti*. Dough cohesiveness was evaluated with the Instron food-testing instrument using a back extrusion cell. Cohesive doughs yielded a characteristic back extruction profile requiring less force for deformation. Poor quality dough that is less cohesive gets compressed into the cell without extrusion extracts of flour on dough stickiness (Plate 7).

The relationship between the physicochemical characters and roti quality indicated that quantity of water-soluble proteins; amylose and sugars jointly influence the roti quality.

The most common use of sorghum in India is in the form of flour or grit, which is transformed into dough and baked on an open hot pan (*Tawa*) as falt unleavened bread i.e. *roti* or *bhakri*. *Bhakri* is the traditional type round pancake made by the traditional method. A large number of diabetic patients are regularly consuming sorghum bhakari with bitter gourd or fenugreek *subji* through every day meals. However, the bhakari consumption has been restricted owing to its coarse nature and palatability. For obtaining good quality bhakari flour, a 60-mesh sieve could be used for separation of the seed coat from the whole flour. However, the whole meal flour is used for the special bhakari making intended for the diabetics and other patients.

Sorghum hybrids, in general are rated low for consumption as compared to local or varieties/cultivars because of numerous consumer complaints. The poor *bhakari* making quality is exemplified by low water-holding capacity of the flour, difficulty in kneading, cracking and low extensibility of dough, crumbling during baking and low water retention.

Procedure for *bhakari* preparation:

Sieve sorghum flour using 60-mesh sieve. Add small quantity of salt if required, hot water and knead into smooth soft dough. Make round small ball approximately 50 or 100 g weight and spread it into a round sheet using rolling pin or by pressing with hand palms or using modern roti making machine. Bake it on pre-heated pan (*Tawa*) or iron sheet. Apply immediately water on the top of bhakari while baking. After that change the up side down and partially bake it on pan/Tawa or iron sheet. Finally place it directly on hot coke or gas flame and bake till we get good puffed bhakari. Such type of bhakari serve immediately hot i.e. fresh. The flow sheet for the preparation of *bhakari/roti* is given in Figure 7. The nutritional composition of *bhakari* is given in Table 47.

Bhakari / Roti (Unleavened Bread)

Sorghum Grains

↓

Cleaning

↓

Grinding

↓

Sieve with 60-mesh sieve (for fine flour if required)

↓

Flour

↓

Add salt and hot water

↓

Knead into smooth dough

↓

Make small balls (50 or 100g)

↓

Roll dough into round pan/iron sheet or
use *bhakari*-making machine to get uniform thickness of *bhakari*

↓

Bake on hot iron pan/Tawa

↓

Apply water on top of *bhakari*

↓

Remove it by flat iron spoon after 2-3 min.

↓

Make upside down and bake sufficiently to form semi hard body

↓

Finally bake it on hot coke or on gas flame

↓

Bhakari puffs into two layers (upper thin and lower thick)

↓

Serve it as hot or cool to room temperature

↓

Store in moisture proof paper or container

↓

Vacuumise it, seal and store for 3 – 4 days
(It remains in good condition)

Figure 7. Flow sheet for preparation of *bhakari* from sorghum and other millets.

Preservation of *bhakari*

The sorghum *bhakari* can be preserved in LDPE bags (200 gauge) or laminated pouches by vacuumization packaging technique. This technique showed that *bhakari* remains soft and retain their palatability upto two days under ambient conditions. The *bhakari* making and preservation technique could be used on commercial scale so as to make it easily available in the market for ready consumption.

Extension shelf life of *bhakari*

Traditionally, the sorghum *bhakari* are consumed as fresh i.e. within eight hours after preparation. Addition of 2 - 3 per cent phosphatised starch or 2 per cent guar gum in the sorghum flour significantly improved the *bhakari* taste and palatability by retaining maximum amount of moisture. Packaging *bhakari/ roti* in laminate pouches after vacuumization found to increase the shelf life by 2 days.

Nutritional and *bhakari* making qualities of some improved cultivars of grain sorghum.

The physical properties, nutritional composition, digestibilities of protein and starch and *bhakari* making quality of some improved sorghum cultivars have been investigated. Both protein and starch digestibilities varied markedly among the cultivars studied. The cultivars M 35 - 1, SPV - 86 and CSH - 8R exhibited superior sensory properties of *bhakari* over other cultivars (Tables 15, 16, 17 and 18). The grain weight, soluble proteins and soluble sugars were found to be positively correlated with *bhakari* quality. These results indicated that certain hybrids are comparable in both nutritional and bhakari quality with varieties. It is suggested that while breeding varieties for higher yields, attention needs to be paid for obtaining higher grain weight, soluble proteins and soluble sugars in the newly developed high yielding cultivars.

Table 15. Physical properties and nutritional quality of different cultivars of grain sorghum.

Cultivar	Grain wt. (g/100seeds)	Grain hardness (kg)	Protein (% N X 6.25) (%)	Soluble proteins (%)	Starch (%)	Reducing sugars (%)	Total sugars (%)	IVPD* (%)	IVSD* (mg maltose/g /2 hr)
Varieties									
M 35 - 1	3.89	6.4	11.90	1.33	76.23	0.14	2.00	69.07	181
CSV - 4	3.52	7.5	13.20	1.30	73.50	0.07	0.86	60.39	200
SPV - 504	4.17	5.9	10.50	1.18	77.24	0.10	0.90	72.86	160
SPV - 351	2.50	8.5	11.77	1.07	75.42	0.08	0.78	78.91	135
SPV - 86	3.81	6.4	10.12	1.15	76.72	0.08	0.87	73.12	168
Hybrids									
CSH - 1	3.34	6.0	9.62	1.15	78.32	0.10	0.81	59.41	150
CSH - 5	3.42	6.8	11.38	1.08	76.81	0.10	1.00	75.07	140
CSH - 6	2.91	6.2	11.38	1.08	76.81	0.10	1.00	67.41	184
CSH - 9	3.53	5.2	10.58	1.19	76.93	0.11	1.24	68.67	140
CSH - 8R	3.19	5.8	10.77	0.98	76.55	0.14	0.96	60.63	166

*IVPD = In-vitro protein digestibility; IVSD = In-vitro starch digestibility.

Table 16. *Bhakari* making quality of different cultivars of grain sorghum.

Cultivar	Water uptake (ml/50 g of flour)	Dough rollability (cm)	Per cent moisture loss in *bhakari* after storage (hrs)			
			3	6	12	24
Varieties						
M 35 - 1	50.7	21.3	0.88	4.98	7.99	17.21
CSV - 4	58.0	22.5	1.53	4.19	7.85	15.02
SPV - 504	53.0	22.9	1.06	5.01	6.80	15.56
SPV - 351	53.0	21.8	2.42	4.97	8.17	16.61
SPV - 86	56.0	22.8	2.07	4.28	7.88	13.89
Hybrids						
CSH - 1	51.7	22.2	1.92	4.49	7.93	15.33
CSH - 5	57.7	22.7	2.73	5.19	8.98	16.69
CSH - 6	53.7	24.5	1.82	5.04	9.88	16.48
CSH - 9	52.7	24.0	1.58	4.41	8.11	15.67
CSH - 8R	52.0	23.3	2.88	5.17	8.64	15.85

Table 17. Sensory properties of sorghum *bhakari.**

Cultivar	Colour and appearance	Texture	Flavour	Sweetness	Mean
Varieties					
M 35 - 1	9.00	8.75	8.00	7.94	8.43
CSV - 4	7.25	7.06	7.50	7.50	7.35
SPV - 504	7.25	7.63	7.69	7.44	7.50
SPV - 351	6.63	6.75	6.38	6.75	6.65
SPV - 86	8.25	7.75	7.63	7.75	7.88
Hybrids					
CSH - 1	3.75	5.88	6.25	6.13	5.53
CSH - 5	6.75	7.38	6.88	7.13	7.05
CSH - 6	7.38	7.25	7.00	7.75	7.38
CSH - 9	7.25	7.75	7.50	7.25	7.48
CSH - 8R	7.75	8.00	7.50	7.75	7.78
S.E. ±	0.28	0.29	0.28	0.31	0.23
CD at 5%	0.79	0.81	0.80	0.89	0.68

*Sensory score out of 10 point hedonic scale using 5 semi-trained judges

Table 18. Correlation coefficient between physico-chemical characters and sensory properties of sorghum *bhakari*.

Character	Colour and appearance	Texture	Flavour	Sweetness	Acceptability
Grain weight	+ 0.722	+ 0.367	+ 0.314	+ 0.476	+ 0.443
Grain hardness	- 0.387	- 0.326	- 0.029	- 0.309	- 0.199
Soluble sugars	+ 0.368	+ 0.353	+ 0.292	+ 0.597	+ 0.398
Soluble proteins	+ 0.484	+ 0.219	+ 0.235	+ 0.232	+ 0.277

Effect of grain conditioning on physico-chemical properties of sorghum *bhakari*:

Sorghum grains conditioned with 10% extra moisture before traditional milling exhibited 9 to 11 per cent removal of bran during household sieving. The resultant flour exhibited improved water absorption during dough preparation and weight of bhakari during storage. The boiling water for dough preparation accentuated this effect. The conditioning and removal of bran did not influence the nutrient composition of bhakari markedly except significant lowering the fiber content. The results indicated that eating quality and storability of sorghum bhakari could be improved by simply conditioning treatment to grains prior to milling without adversely affecting the nutritional composition. Effect of processing on the nutritional and other parameters are given in Tables 19, 20, 21, and 22.

Table 19. Effect of conditioning the grains on the removal of bran.

Conditioning moisture (%)	Per cent bran removed*		
	M 35 – 1	CSH - 5	CSH – 8R
10 (control)	5.0	4.4	4.4
15 (5% extra)	8.0	8.4	7.4
20 (10% extra)	11.6	10.4	9.6

*Means of duplicate experiments

Table 20. Effect of conditioning the grains on water absorption by resultant flour.

Conditioning moisture (%)	Water temperature for dough preparation (^0C)	Per cent water absorption*		
		M 35 -1	CSH - 5	CSH –8R
10 (control)	25	82	86	82
20 (10% extra)	25	94	92	92
10 (control)	50	86	90	86
20 (10% extra)	50	94	94	94
10 (control)	Boiling water	90	96	88
20 (10% extra)	Boiling water	104	98	100

*Means of duplicate experiments.

Effect of incorporation of wheat, maize, black gram, and defatted soybean flour in sorghum flour on physical and sensory properties of *bhakari*:

Mixing of wheat, maize, black gram and defatted soybean flour to sorghum flour resulted in the decrease in water absorption by the flour during dough making, decreased the fresh weight and increase water loss in *bhakari* during storage. However, the differences in the fresh weight of *bhakari* were not of significant order. Wheat can be mixed to the extent of 10 per cent while maize, black gram and defatted soybean can be mixed to the extent of 20 per cent with sorghum to produce acceptable *bhakari* with improved protein and ash contents. An increase in protein content in such *bhakari* ranged from 8.15 to 17.66 per cent when black gram and defatted sorghum were mixed. The detail data of the experiment is given in Tables 23, 24, 25, 26 and 27.

Table 21. Loss in weight of *bhakari* prepared by using cold (25 ^{0}C) and boiling water during storage.

Cultivar	Conditioning moisture level (%)	Dry weight of bhakari (g) during storage (hrs)									
		Cold water					Boiling water				
		0	3	6	12	24	0	3	6	12	24
M 35-1	10 (control)	78.00	74.75 (4.2)	74.25 (4.8)	73.50 (5.8)	72.75 (6.7)	81.00	76.00 (6.2)	75.00 (7.4)	73.50 (9.3)	70.50 (12.4)
	20 (10% extra)	84.00	79.75 (5.1)	79.00 (6.0)	78.00 (7.1)	75.90 (9.6)	88.00	82.75 (6.0)	81.75 (7.1)	80.00 (9.1)	78.50 (11.9)
CSH-5	10 (control)	80.00	76.00 (5.0)	75.50 (5.6)	74.50 (6.9)	73.00 (8.8)	84.00	79.00 (6.9)	78.00 (7.1)	77.00 (8.3)	76.00 (9.5)
	20 (10% extra)	83.00	79.75 (4.0)	79.00 (4.8)	78.25 (5.7)	76.75 (8.1)	85.00	81.00 (4.7)	80.00 (5.9)	79.00 (7.1)	78.00 (8.2)
CSH-8R	10 (control)	78.00	74.50 (4.5)	74.00 (5.1)	73.50 (5.8)	72.00 (7.7)	80.00	77.00 (3.8)	76.00 (5.0)	75.00 (6.3)	74.00 (7.6)
	20 (10% extra)	83.00	79.00 (4.8)	78.50 (5.4)	78.00 (6.0)	75.50 (9.0)	86.00	82.00 (4.7)	81.00 (5.8)	79.75 (7.3)	77.25 (10.2)

*Figures in parentheses indicate per cent weight loss

Table 22. Proximate composition of *bhakari* prepared from different resultant flours.

Cultivar	Conditioning moisture level (%)	Protein (%)	Crude fat (%)	Crude fiber (%)	Ash (%)	N-Free extract (%)
M 35 - 1	10 (Control)	10.55	3.51	2.05	1.77	82.12
	20 (10% extra)	10.41	3.27	0.80	1.58	83.94
CSH - 5	10 (Control)	9.02	3.61	1.95	1.58	83.84
	20 (10% extra)	8.95	2.76	0.89	1.55	85.85
CSH -8R	10 (Control)	8.94	3.26	1.95	1.80	84.05
	20 (10% extra)	8.89	3.17	0.72	1.72	85.50

Table 23. Sensory properties of *bhakari* prepared from sorghum:wheat flour blends

Flour blend, % Sorghum: Wheat	Colour & appearance	Flavour	Texture and body	Sweetness	Overall acceptability
100:O	7.75	8.00	8.25	8.25	8.06
90:10	7.00	7.50	7.61	7.25	7.34
80:20	6.75	7.27	7.25	7.25	7.13
70:30	6.50	7.25	7.25	7.25	7.06
S.E. ±	0.24	0.23	0.28	0.20	0.24
CD at 5%	0.77	0.76	0.89	0.66	0.77

Table 24. Sensory properties of *bhakari* prepared from sorghum:maize flour blends.

Flour blend, % Sorghum:Maize	Colour & appearance	Flavour	Texture and body	Sweetness	Overall acceptability
100:0	7.75	8.00	8.25	8.25	8.06
90:10	8.50	7.25	7.00	8.00	7.68
80:20	7.90	7.20	7.00	7.50	7.40
70:30	7.00	6.75	6.75	7.25	6.94
S.E. ±	0.18	0.17	0.24	0.24	0.21
CD at 5%	0.57	0.54	0.77	0.77	0.66

Table 25. Sensory properties of *bhakari* prepared from sorghum : black gram flour blends.

Flour blend, % Sorghum : Black gram	Colour & appearance	Flavour	Texture and body	Sweetness	Overall acceptability
100:O	8.50	8.25	8.25	8.50	8.38
90:10	8.25	8.00	7.50	7.75	7.88
80:20	7.75	8.00	7.50	7.25	7.63
70:30	7.50	7.50	7.25	6.50	7.19
S.E. ±	0.31	0.21	0.34	0.24	0.28
CD at 5%	1.02	0.68	1.12	0.77	0.90

Table 26. Sensory properties of *bhakari* prepared from sorghum : soybean flour blends.

Flour blend, % Sorghum: Soybean	Colour & appearance	Flavour	Texture and body	Sweetness	Overall acceptability
100:O	8.50	8.25	8.25	8.50	8.38
90:10	8.00	7.75	8.25	8.25	8.06
80:20	8.75	7.75	8.00	8.25	7.69
70:30	6.50	7.00	6.50	7.00	6.75
S.E. ±	0.36	0.27	0.20	0.33	0.29
CD at 5%	1.16	0.87	0.66	1.05	0.94

Utilization of groundnut flour in preparation of sorghum *bhakari / roti*.

Sorghum is consumed as one of the staple food grains in India. It is mostly consumed in the form of unleavened traditional products, *bhakari* and *sankati*. However, these products are low in protein content and exhibit poor sensory properties, which limit the acceptability of sorghum, particularly, that of high yielding hybrids by the consumers. The defatted oilseed flours contain 40 to 60% proteins and thus form a potential protein source to the vegetarian diets. Such flours can be supplemented with low-protein cereals meals to facilitate their utilization in human foods and also to improve the protein content of cereal-based foods. An attempt has been therefore, made to supplement sorghum meal with 10 to 30% defatted groundnut flour in the preparation of sorghum *bhakari* and to study its acceptability.

Table 27. Proximate composition of *bhakari* prepared from various composite flours.

Sample	Protein (%)	Crude fat (%)	Crude fiber (%)	Ash (%)	N-free extract (%)
Sorghum (CSH-5, 100%)	8.15	3.31	0.80	1.55	86.19
Flour blends					
Sorghum : Wheat					
0:100	14.07	2.46	1.06	1.70	80.71
90:10	10.26	2.70	1.40	1.52	84.12
80:20	11.49	2.82	1.33	1.54	82.82
70:30	12.64	2.95	1.28	1.60	81.53
Sorghum:Maize					
0:100	11.96	4.30	0.75	2.58	80.41
90:10	8.49	3.00	0.76	1.70	86.05
80:20	9.27	3.32	0.72	1.88	84.81
70:30	9.68	3.60	0.70	2.02	84.00
Sorghum:Blackgram					
0:100	22.09	2.03	0.10	3.32	72.46
90:10	10.43	2.50	0.75	1.85	84.47
80:20	12.00	2.33	0.70	2.03	82.94
70:30	12.73	2.19	0.65	2.32	82.11
Sorghum:Soybean					
0:100	53.46	4.20	4.57	5.82	31.95
90:10	12.68	2.94	1.60	2.24	80.54
80:20	17.66	3.00	2.35	2.85	74.14
70:30	21.79	3.25	3.21	3.34	68.41

The defatted groundnut flour (prepared in the laboratory by solvent extraction of full-fat meal) was blended with sorghum flour (cv. CSH – 9) in the proportion of 0, 10, 20, and 30% (w/w). The water uptake by the composite flour, dough rollability and moisture loss from *bhakari* during storage were studied. Fresh *bhakari* was evaluated by panel of judges for various sensory properties such as colour and appearance, flavour, texture, and sweetness using 10-point hedonic scale. Average of five judges were used to determine the acceptability of the product.

Mixing of defatted groundnut flour with sorghum flour to the extent of 20 to 30% significantly decreased the water uptake by the flour during dough preparation. However, the rollability of dough and the per cent water loss from the *bhakari* during storage upto 12 hrs were not significantly affected. Blending of groundnut flour to the extent of 30% significantly improved colour and appearance, texture and sweetness of sorghum *bhakari*. The flavour of composite *bhakari* was not significantly affected by addition of defatted groundnut flour. The results indicated that mixing of groundnut flour significantly improved the overall sensory properties and acceptability of sorghum *bhakari*.

Mixing of 30% of defatted groundnut flour containing about 40% proteins with 70g of sorghum flour containing 10% proteins, would give composite flour with about 19% protein content. Moreover, the composite *bhakari* is more acceptable than the product prepared from 100% sorghum flour (Table 28).

Table. 28. Physical and sensory properties of *bhakari* prepared from sorghum:groundnut composite flour.

Flour blend (w/w) Sorghum:Groundnut	Water uptake (ml/50g of flour)	Dough rollability (cm)	Water loss during storage 12 hrs, (%)	Sensory qualities of sorghum *bhakari*				
				Colour & appearance	Flavour	Texture	Sweetness	Overall mean
100:0	50.00	20.00	11.62	8.00	7.80	7.80	8.00	7.90
90:10	48.50	20.15	11.91	7.40	7.20	7.40	7.80	7.45
80:20	42.00	20.30	11.67	8.60	7.80	8.40	8.40	8.30
70:30	41.00	20.00	12.90	8.80	8.20	8.80	9.00	8.70
CD at 5%	1.72	N.S.	N.S.	0.52	0.62	0.53	0.38	0.56

N.S. = Non-Significant

Chapter 12

Nutritional Improvement and Utilization of Grain Sorghum by Fermentation

A natural lactic fermentation of ground grain sorghum produced significant increase ($P < 0.001$) in available lysine/leucine, isoleucine, and methionine. The protein quality, expressed as relative nutritive value, increased significantly ($P <0.001$) as a result of fermentation. Niacin and thiamine increased significantly ($P <0.001$) and riboflavin also increased ($P < 0.05$) during the fermentation (Table 29). Protein and carbohydrate appeared to be more available after the fermentation than before the fermentation. Although the fermentation produced increased availability of nutrients, it did not produce change in the proximate analyses.

The relative nutritive value (% RNV) of sorghum fermented at 25 ^{0}C and 35 ^{0}C increased significantly ($P < 0.05$) over the % RNV of the control. During the consecutive 7-day fermentation at 25 ^{00}C, time had no effect on the % RNV. The highest % RNV (56.45%) was achieved at the end of 1 day. Fermentation at 35 ^{0}C was influenced by the time, with the highest % RNV (61.11%) obtained at the end of 7 days. Available lysine and methionine increased substantially ($P < 0.01$) over the control when sorghum was fermented at 25 ^{0}C or 35 ^{0}C for 4 days. Sorghum fermented at 25 ^{0}C and at 35 ^{0}C had methionine content of 25.68 and 26.79 mg/g N, respectively, whereas the control contained only 11.25 mg/g N. Lysine level were 33.2 and 34.5 mg/g N in sorghum fermented at 25 ^{0}C and 35 ^{0}C, respectively, whereas the control contained 9.1 mg/g N. None of the available B-vitamins studied was altered significantly in the fermented samples (Table 30.).

The grain sorghum is mainly consumed as *bhakari* and it is an age-old food habit of the sorghum consumers in India. Any improvement in the cultivar for making better quality bhakari will be appreciated. Considering the nutritional and evident quality problems of grain sorghum, the malting or fermentation of the whole sorghum flour for making bread, pancake, and other breakfast foods hold good promise of improving the functionality and utilization of sorghum as staple food by all classes of people in India. However, the utilization of sorghum in the form of beer or table wine seems to be uneconomical in comparison to the whole flour due to social and psychological food habits, low amylopectic power of sorghum malt and significant loss of solids during the beer making process.

According to Novellie (1968) the beer-making process may depend upon two fermentations involving (1) bacteria that produce lactic acid, (2) yeasts that produce alcohol. The malting process that generates the fermentable mono and disaccharides is depending upon the α- and β–amylases and the maltose splitting enzyme, maltase, that develops in the sorghum during germination. The beer is sour due to the presence of lactic acid (pH 3.3 to 3.5), opaque because of suspended solids and yeast, and lightly alcoholic due to 3 to 3.5 per cent alcohol by mass. Sorghum beers differ in many ways from barley beer (Table 31). The nutritional value of sorghum beer is higher than that of most other beers because of the yeasts and other suspended material. The beer made from highly refined maize (adjunct) and unrefined sorghum malt has a lower vitamin value than that made from the same malt with ground whole sorghum grains as adjunct (Table 32). *Amgba* and *affouk* contained, respectively 20 to 31 per cent of the original sorghum solids. It was concluded that consumption of sorghum flour is more economical than that of sorghum beer or wine in terms of calories and proteins (Table 33).

Table 29. Composition of non-fermented and fermented sorghum meals*.

Constituent	Non-fermented	Fermented	Significance between meals
Proximate analysis (%)			
Crude protein	10.2	14.48	NS
Crude fiber	2.45	2.35	NS
Crude fat	3.13	3.20	NS
Ash	1.56	1.40	NS
Carbohydrates	82.84	82.57	NS
Available amino acids (mg/gN)			
Lysine	23.40	40.34	P < 0.001
Leucine	27.50	59.38	P < 0.001
Isoleucine	38.67	81.62	P < 0.001
Methionine	15.98	33.35	P < 0.001
% RNV	70.00	83.72	P < 0.001
Protein digestibility (%)			
With papain	1.42	8.33	P < 0.005
Without papain	1.36	8.21	P < 0.005
Carbohydrate availability (%)			
Reducing sugars	0.19	0.42	P < 0.001
Starch (with takadiastase)	16.70	31.82	P < 0.001
Starch (without takadiastase)	1.36	8.21	P < 0.001
Vitamins (mg/g)			
Niacin	37.90	41.30	P < 0.001
Thiamine	20.20	47.10	P < 0.001
Riboflavin	0.90	1.30	P < 0.005

*Means of four replications. Source: Kazanas and Fields, 1981.

Table 30. Nutritional processing quality of sorghum.

Nutrients	Sorghum meal		
		Fermented	
	Control	25 °C	35 °C
Methionine (mg/gN)	9.1a*	33.2b	34.5b
Lysine (mg/gN)	11.25 a*	25.68b	26.79b
Thiamin (mg/gN)	3.66ab*	3.18b	3.87b
Riboflavin (mg/gN)	1.34a*	1.27a	1.38a
Niacin (mg/gN)	68.39a**	70.88a	70.91a
% RNV	45.57**	55.10a	56.17a

N = 5, Means with different letters are significantly different.
*Significant at $P<0.01$; **Significant at $P < 0.05$; Source: Au and Field, 1981.

Table 31. Composition of sorghum beer with that of European Barley Beer.

Beer	Raw materials used			Fermentation process	
	Malt	Adjunct	Hops	Lactic	Alcoholic
Sorghum	Sorghum malt	Maize or sorghum	None	+	+
European	Barley malt	Cereals or syrups	+	-	+

Source: Novellie, 1977.

Table 32. Vitamin content (mg/100 g) of sorghum beer.

Vitamin	1975 Maize as adjunct	1976 Sorghum as adjunct	1972	1973
Thiamine	27	47	35	32
Niacin	222	400	270	189
Riboflavin	27	35	27	36

Source: Novellie, 1977.

Table 33. Comparison of nutritional composition of sifted flour, *amgba* and *affouk* as % of whole grain.

Composition	Sorghum	Sifted flour	*Amgba*	*Affouk* wine
Solids	100	70	20	31
Calories (Alcohol not included)	100	75	20	33
Total calories (Alcohol included)	100	75	29	55
Protein	100	69	19	41
Lysine	100	-	41	56
Lipid	100	35	0	28
Total carbohydrates	100	72	19	29
Cellulose	100	28	0	12
Ash	100	39	36	42
Calcium	100	59	35	81
Total P	100	41	38	65
Phytic P	100	-	13	47
Thiamine	100	39	160	65
Riboflavin	100	34	145	141
Niacin	100	30	35	41

Source: Chevassus-Agnes *et al.*, (1976)

Effect of fermentation on soluble proteins and *in-vitro* protein digestibility of sorghum, green gram and sorghum + green gram blends.

Sorghum seeds (cv. M 35 –1) were obtained from the Senior Sorghum Breeder, MPKV, Rahuri and the green gram (*Vigna radiata*) seeds were purchased from the local market. Grains were separately milled to 60 mesh and mixed (70:30, w/w) to obtain composite meal. The meals were mixed with water (1:3, w/v) and natural fermentation was carried out up to 5 days at 25 °C in beakers covered with aluminium foil. Sorbic acid (0.1% in meal) was used to prevent mold growth during fermentation. The pH of the fermenting material was measured with Elico-pH meter while the titratable acidity expressed as per cent lactic acid, was determined by titration with 0.1N NaOH. The slurries were dried in petri dishes at 55 ^{0}C to constant weight and powdered. The dried meals were analyzed for crude protein, soluble proteins, free amino acids and in-vitro protein digestibility.

Fermentation at 25 ^{0}C upto 5 days were monitored and changes in pH, titratable acidity and proteins of meals of sorghum, green gram and sorghum + green gram blend (70:30, w/w) were studied. The pH of fermenting meals decreased sharply with concomitant increase in the titratable acidity within 24 hrs. The proteins, free amino acids, soluble proteins and in-vitro protein digestibility markedly increased within 24 hrs fermentation (Table 34 and 35). Supplementation of green gram with sorghum decreased the acidity and improved the contents of crude protein, soluble proteins and free amino acids of fermented sorghum meal.

Table 34. Effect of fermentation on pH, acidity and protein of sorghum, green gram and sorghum-green gram blend.

Fermentation period (days)	PH			Titratable acidity (%)			Protein (N x 6.25) (%)		
	Sorghum	Green gram	Sorghum + green gram	Sorghum	Green gram	Sorghum + green gram	Sorghum	Green gram	Sorghum + green gram
Control	6.3	5.9	6.1	0.11	0.33	0.14	11.4	24.6	14.9
1	4.3	4.5	4.1	0.44	0.43	0.46	12.8	26.8	17.0
2	3.7	4.3	3.9	1.01	0.44	0.62	13.1	27.0	17.2
3	3.6	4.3	3.8	1.15	0.45	0.79	13.2	27.2	17.6
4	3.5	4.3	3.7	1.27	0.46	0.86	13.5	26.6	17.1
5	3.5	4.2	3.7	1.36	0.47	1.00	13.6	26.5	16.8

Table 35. Effect of fermentation on soluble proteins, free amino acids and in-vitro protein digestibility of sorghum, green gram and sorghum-green gram blend.

Fermentation period (days)	Soluble proteins (%)			Free amino acids (mg/g meal)			IVPD (%)		
	Sorghum	Green gram	Sorghum + green gram	Sorghum	Green gram	Sorghum + green gram	Sorghum	Green gram	Sorghum + green gram
Control	1.4	11.7	5.1	2.6	4.8	2.7	80.2	82.0	80.8
1	2.1	15.3	6.2	6.9	22.4	12.5	85.8	87.0	86.2
2	2.1	15.3	6.4	7.1	23.2	14.8	85.4	87.1	86.3
3	2.1	16.2	6.3	7.5	23.5	14.9	87.4	87.2	86.4
4	2.1	15.8	6.5	7.9	24.0	15.8	86.9	87.9	87.3
5	2.1	15.5	6.1	8.2	25.1	17.8	85.7	88.3	86.4

Chapter 13

Effect of Malting and Fermentation on Nutritional Quality of Sorghum

The grains of sorghum cultivars M 35 –1 and Swati and CSH – 5 were steeped in water for 10 hrs, germinated at 30 ^{0}C for 24 hrs in incubator, dried at 60 ^{0}C to constant weight and milled to 60 mesh. For fermentation studies the grains were milled to 60 mesh, mixed with distilled water (1:3, w/v) containing 0.1% sorbic acid to prevent mold growth and fermented in beakers covered with aluminium foil for 24 hrs at 25 ^{0}C. The slurries were dried to constant weight at 60 ^{0}C. The dried meals were analyzed for crude protein, free amino acids, water soluble proteins, starch, in-vitro protein digestibility and loss in dry weight was measured by weighing the dry meals before and after malting or fermentation.

Both malting and fermentation treatments markedly improved the nutritional quality of sorghum (Plate 8 and Table 36). The reducing sugars, free amino acids and protein digestibility were found to be increased after malting of grains for 24 hrs. Malting however, did not affect the contents of crude or soluble proteins. The fermentation of meals for 24 hrs markedly increased both the crude and soluble proteins along with reducing sugars, free amino acids and protein digestibility. Natural fermentation of meal appears to be superior processing technique over malting in improving the nutritional quality of grain sorghum. The loss in dry matter both during malting and fermentation was higher in CSH – 5 than Swati and M 35 – 1.

Table 36. Effect of malting and fermentation on nutritional quality of sorghum cultivars.

Parameter/Cultivars /Malting/Fermentation period	M 35 - 1		Swati		CSH - 5	
A. Malting	0	24	0	24	0	24
Malting loss, %	-	3.2	-	2.9	-	3.8
Crude protein, %	11.6	11.6	10.7	10.7	11.3	11.3
Soluble proteins, %	1.2	1.0	0.9	0.9	1.0	0.9
Free amino acids, mg/g	2.2	3.3	1.7	3.3	1.8	2.6
Starch, %	69.5	68.0	68.2	67.0	68.4	66.3
Reducing sugars, %	0.2	1.4	0.1	0.7	0.1	1.4
IVPD, %	80.8	82.7	81.6	84.7	78.5	79.2
B. Fermentation						
Dry matter loss, %	-	1.6	-	4.4	-	6.6
Crude protein, %	11.4	12.8	11.7	13.2	10.2	11.8
Free amino acids, mg/g	2.6	6.9	1.7	6.2	1.7	6.3
Soluble proteins, %	1.4	2.1	1.4	2.1	1.1	2.0
Starch, %	76.3	74.0	72.1	69.5	74.4	73.5
Reducing sugars, %	0.3	4.1	0.2	3.1	0.2	3.2
IVPD, %	80.2	85.8	79.4	87.4	78.6	84.6

Utilization of malted sorghum, mung bean and black gram in preparation of *bhakari / roti*:

The grains of sorghum (CSH – 5), mung bean and black gram were malted for 24 hrs at 27 °C, dried at 60 °C and milled to 60 mesh. The meals of malted grains were separately blended with normal sorghum flour at different proportions. The *bhakari* were prepared from 50g of such composite meal. The fresh *bhakaries* were evaluated for their sensory properties by the semi-trained judges using 10-point hedonic scale. The average score values given by 5 judges were used to determine acceptability of the product.

Blending of the meal of malted sorghum with normal flour to the extent of 80% lowered the flavour and enhanced the sweetness of *bhakari*. Blending of malted mung bean flour to the extent of 30% with sorghum produced acceptable *bhakari* with significant improvement in sweetness as compared with unmalted mung bean:Sorghum blend. Similar results were also obtained with unmalted and malted black gram (Table 37). An improvement in sweetness of the product can be attributed to the increased sugar levels in malted meals. The results indicate that malted sorghum to the extent of 80% and mung bean or black gram to the level of 30% can be blended with normal sorghum flour to obtain acceptable *bhakari* with improved nutritional value.

Table 37. Sensory qualities of *bhakari* prepared from sorghum meal supplemented with malted sorghum, mung bean and black gram flour.

Flour blend (w/w)	Colour and appearance	Flavour	Texture	Taste/ Sweetness	Overall mean
Sorghum:Malted sorghum					
100:0	7.0	7.3	7.7	7.5	7.4
80:20	6.5	6.2	7.0	7.7	6.9
60:40	7.0	6.5	7.2	7.7	7.1
40:60	6.5	6.3	7.3	7.7	7.0
20:80	6.8	6.3	7.5	8.0	7.2
S. E. ±	N.S.	N.S.	N.S.	N.S.	N.S.
Sorghum:Normal mung bean					
100:0	8.3	8.1	8.3	8.5	8.3
90:10	8.3	8.1	7.8	7.5	7.9
80:20	7.9	8.2	7.4	7.4	7.7
70:30	7.4	7.6	7.3	7.1	7.4
CD at 5%	N.S.	N.S.	N.S.	N.S.	N.S.
Sorghum:Malted mung bean					
100:0	8.0	8.0	8.0	8.1	8.0
90:10	8.0	7.8	7.8	8.1	7.9
80:20	7.8	7.4	7.6	8.1	7.7
70:30	7.8	7.8	7.6	8.1	7.8
S. E. ±	N.S.	N.S.	N.S.	N.S.	N.S.
Sorghum:Normal black gram					
100:0	8.5	8.2	8.3	8.5	8.4
90:10	8.3	8.0	7.5	7.8	7.9
80:20	7.8	8.0	7.5	7.3	7.7
70:30	7.5	7.5	7.3	6.5	7.2
CD at 5%	N.S.	N.S.	N.S.	N.S.	N.S.

Sorghum:Malted black gram					
100:0	7.6	7.6	7.4	7.4	7.5
90:10	7.6	7.8	7.8	7.6	7.7
80:20	7.8	8.0	8.0	8.2	8.0
70:30	8.0	7.6	8.0	8.4	8.0
S.E. ±	N.S.	N.S.	N.S.	N.S.	N.S.

N.S. = Non-significant

Effect of malting on proximate composition and *in-vitro* protein digestibility and starch digestibility of grain sorghum:

The changes in dry matter, nutrient composition and *in-vitro* protein and starch digestibilities were studied during malting of grain sorghum. The steeping of grains in water for 10 to 30 hrs and germinating at 30 °C upto 72 hrs significantly decreased the dry weight and starch while significantly increasing the water soluble proteins, free amino acids and reducing sugars in malted meal (Table 38 and 39). The steeping of grains for 10 hrs and subsequent germination for 24 hrs significantly improved *in-vitro* protein and starch digestibility of the malted meal. However, prolonged steeping or germination of grains exhibited adverse effects on the digestibility of starch. The results indicated that 10 hrs steeping followed by 24 hrs germination is optimum to produce sorghum malt for traditional food uses.

Table 38. Effect of malting on malting loss (%) and proximate composition of sorghum.

Composition	Steeping period (hr)	Malting period (hr)		
		24	48	72
Malting loss (%)	10	3.2	11.2	19.5
	20	6.2	13.6	20.9
	30	9.5	17.5	25.6
Crude protein (%) (11.6)	10	11.6	11.3	11.2
	20	10.6	10.5	10.1
	30	10.2	10.2	9.9
Crude fat (%) (4.0)	10	4.0	3.0	3.0
	20	4.1	3.2	2.8
	30	4.2	3.2	2.6

Crude fiber (%) (1.8)	10 20 30	2.0 1.9 1.8	1.8 1.8 1.7	1.7 1.8 1.6
Ash (%) (1.7)	10 20 30	1.0 1.0 1.2	1.0 0.9 1.0	1.0 0.9 1.0

LSD at 5%, Malting loss = 0.05; Protein = 0.3; fat, fiber and ash = 0.2.
Figures in parentheses represent the composition of unmalted dry grain.

Table 39. Effect of malting on soluble proteins, free amino acids, starch, reducing sugars and in-vitro protein and starch digestibilities in sorghum.

Constituent	Steeping period (hr)	Malting period (hr)		
		24	48	72
Soluble proteins (%) (1.2)	10 20 30	1.2 1.3 1.9	1.6 1.9 2.3	1.9 2.4 2.8
Free amino acids (mg/g) (2.2)	10 20 30	3.3 3.5 5.8	5.9 6.5 7.8	7.1 8.1 10.2
Starch (%) (69.5)	10 20 30	68.0 64.3 62.3	60.5 55.1 50.5	57.6 53.1 49.1
Reducing sugars (%) (0.2)	10 20 30	1.4 1.7 2.6	2.7 3.7 4.7	4.8 6.4 7.3
IVPD (%) (80.8)	10 20 30	82.7 79.5 78.4	85.3 80.9 79.4	90.2 83.4 83.8
IVSD (mg maltose/g/2 hr) (137.1)	10 20 30	204.0 136.4 121.4	125.7 124.7 78.5	97.1 76.0 60.7

LSD at 5%, Soluble proteins = 0.2; Free amino acid = 3.2; starch = 2.8; Reducing sugars = 0.2; IVPD = 2.5; IVSD = 2.8.
Figures in parentheses represent the composition of unmalted dry grain.

Chapter **14**

Supplementing Sorghum Flour with Wheat Maida

Effect of incorporation of sorghum flour in wheat maida on physical and sensory properties of bread, buns, cookies and biscuits.

Bread, sweet buns, cookies and orange biscuits were prepared from the composite flour of wheat and sorghum. The products were evaluated for their physical and sensory properties. The results revealed that sorghum flour with 80% extraction could be mixed with maida to the extent of 20% (w/w) to prepare acceptable bread and buns and to the extent of 30% (w/w) to prepare acceptable cookies and biscuits without using any other additives (Plate 9, and 10, Table 40, 41 and 42).

Table 40. Sensory properties of bread, sweet buns, cookies and orange biscuits prepared from wheat : sorghum blends.

Product/ Blend	Flavour	Crust colour	Crumb or texture	Taste (Sweetness)	Overall acceptability	Spread factor (w/t)
Bread wheat:sorghum						
100:0	8.00	8.50	9.50	9.50	8.88	-
90:10	7.50	8.00	6.50	7.50	7.38	-
80:20	7.50	7.00	6.50	7.00	7.00	-
70:30	5.50	6.50	4.50	5.00	5.38	-
S. E. ±	0.24	0.41	0.36	0.28	0.32	-
CD at 5%	0.78	1.33	1.18	0.90	1.05	-
Sweet buns						
100:0	8.00	8.00	8.00	8.00	8.00	-
90:10	8.00	8.00	8.00	8.00	8.00	-
80:20	7.50	8.00	6.50	8.00	7.50	-
70:30	6.00	6.50	6.00	6.50	6.26	-
S. E. ±	0.13	0.13	0.13	0.13	0.13	-
CD at 5%	0.41	0.41	0.41	0.41	0.41	-

Cookies						
100:0	7.70	7.25	7.35	7.30	7.40	6.45
90:10	6.75	6.75	7.25	7.00	6.94	6.62
80:20	6.25	6.25	6.50	6.75	6.44	6.70
70:30	5.85	6.50	6.50	6.75	6.40	6.71
60:40	3.50	6.00	5.00	6.00	5.13	6.48
50:50	3.00	6.00	5.50	5.75	5.06	6.47
40:60	3.00	6.00	5.25	5.50	4.94	6.44
S. E. ±	0.44	0.30	0.35	0.35	0.36	0.013
CD at 5%	1.32	0.90	1.04	1.06	1.08	0.040
Orange biscuits						
100:0	7.50	7.75	7.25	7.50	7.50	8.40
90:10	6.75	7.50	7.25	7.50	7.25	8.61
80:20	6.25	6.75	6.50	7.50	6.75	8.70
70:30	6.20	6.75	6.25	7.50	6.68	8.80
S. E. ±	0.35	0.29	0.26	0.24	0.29	0.007
CD at 5%	1.15	0.94	0.86	0.77	0.93	0.023

Table 41. Physical properties of the bread and sweet buns prepared from wheat:sorghum blends.

Product/ Blend	Volume (ml)	Vol./Wt. (ratio)	Weight of bread (g) during storage period			
Bread Wheat : Sorghum			O hr	24 hrs	48 hrs	72 hrs
100:0	960	2.65	362.00	346.50 (4.3)	346.00 (4.4)	344.80 (4.8)
90:10	945	2.60	363.00	347.50 (4.3)	347.00 (4.4)	345.50 (4.8)
80:20	905	2.46	367.80	353.00 (4.0)	349.00 (5.1)	346.00 (5.9)
70:30	900	2.43	370.00	356.00 (3.8)	351.00 (5.1)	349.50 (6.5)
Sweet buns Wheat: Sorghum						
100:0	140.50	3.07	45.70	45.00 (1.5)	44.80 (2.0)	43.90 (3.9)
90:10	140.00	2.99	46.90	46.00 (1.9)	45.70 (2.6)	45.00 (4.1)
80:20	132.00	2.78	47.50	47.00 (1.1)	46.60 (1.9)	45.20 (4.8)
70:30	130.00	2.68	48.50	48.00 (1.0)	47.00 (3.1)	46.80 (3.5)

Figures in brackets indicate per cent loss in weight during storage period.

Table 42. Protein and ash contents of the bakery products prepared from wheat:sorghum blends (dry weight basis).

Products	Protein (%)	Ash (%)
Bread		
Sorghum 100%	5.60	0.89
Wheat:Sorghum		
100:0	11.80	2.83
90:10	11.18	2.63
80:20	11.42	2.55
70:30	9.51	2.40
Sweet buns Wheat:Sorghum		
100:0	9.13	1.80
90:10	9.10	1.75
80:20	8.00	1.72
70:30	7.90	1.71
Cookies Wheat:Sorghum		
100:0	6.19	2.09
90:10	5.33	1.74
80:20	4.95	1.64
70:30	4.95	1.54
60:40	4.57	1.40
50:50	4.19	1.33
40:60	4.10	1.30
Orange biscuits Wheat:Sorghum		
100:0	7.23	1.87
90:10	6.85	1.50
80:20	6.60	1.39
70:30	6.20	1.31

Chapter **15**

Convenience Foods from Sorghum

Alternative foods such as ready-to-cook mixes, infant and weaning foods, breakfast foods, snack foods, dehydrated products, flaked products, baked products and popped products can be prepared using sorghum flour and their semolina.

Chapter **16**

Infant Food Mixes/Weaning Foods

Ready-to-cook, *idli* and *dosa* mixes can be developed using sorghum flour. The details of the composite mixes available in the market and infant mixes tested in the research field are given in Table 43 and 44.

Table 43. Composition of *idli* and *dosa* mixes commercially available in the market.

Idli mix ingredients	Per cent	Dosa mix ingredients	Per cent
Dehulled sorghum (rava)	61 (40 mesh)	Sorghum flour	30 (60 mesh)
Black gram dal flour	30.5	Rice flour	30 (60 mesh)
Salt	3	Black gram dal flour	30
Sodium bicarbonate	2	Salt	3.3
Citric acid	2.7	Citric acid	3.85
Sodium acetate	0.65	Calcium carbonate	1.95

Infant and weaning mixes can be prepared using various types of legumes, which balance the nutritional requirement of the growing children. Some of the mixes/formulations, which were tested, are given below.

Table 44. Tested formulations of infant mixes.

Infant mix	Proportion of ingredients
Sorghum soya mix Sorghum rava:soybean flour:SMP	70:25:5
Sorghum soya mix Sorghum flour:soybean flour:sugar	70:10:20
Sorghum pigeonpea mix Sorghum flour:pigeonpea flour	80:20
Pearl millet pulse mix Pearl millet flour:green gram flour Pearl millet flour:blackgram flour Pearl millet:Bengal gram flour	 70:30 70:30 70:30

Weaning foods are intended to supplement the diets of young children when breast milk is no longer sufficient in quantity and to serve as a bridge between breast milk and the daily diet of the young child. There are many commercial preparations available for feeding infants as weaning food. While formulating weaning foods, the nutrient requirements of the child should be taken into consideration. Children need proportionately more protein in relation to their calorie requirement because of their added protein needs for growth. Further, the infections, which are very common among underprivileged children of developing countries, increase their requirements for protein.

Attention must be given in weaning foods to the B-complex vitamins, particularly thiamine, riboflavin and niacin. Pyridoxine is usually adequate unless destroyed in processing. Folic acid, B_{12} may also sometimes need to be considered. Vitamin D is usually available in tropical countries because of the availability of sunlight. Minerals, iron and calcium must also be added. Iodine is essential for the proper functioning of the thyroid gland in the absence of which goiter develops. There must be some fat and oil in the diet to provide a small amount of linoleic acid.

For complete and proper utilization of the weaning foods, the nutrients should be present in the proportion required by the infants. An international agreement has been reached on the minimal compositional standards. The standards prescribed by the Codex Alimentarius Committee on Foods for Dietary Uses for complete infant food are presented in Table 45. It has been tentatively agreed that the maximum levels of nutrients shall be twice the minimum levels except for vitamin D. The vitamin levels are based on the recommendation of the Nutrition Committee of the National American Academy of Pediatrics, which, in turn, are based on levels found in human milk. It is, further, recommended that the proteins should be nutritionally equivalent to that of whole egg, i.e., the biological value should not be less than 70. In case of nutritionally poor proteins, the quantity is increased in proportion to their biological value. However, the maximum protein content should not exceed 3 g/100 K calories. The biological value of protein may be increased by addition of essential amino acids.

In India, the Central Food Technological Research Institute, Mysore, has developed a nutritious children's food called "Bal-Ahar" (Table 46). It is prepared by blending cereals (corn meal, wheat flour) and legumes (soy bean flour, groundnut flour, Bengal gram flour) in certain proportions with or without skim milk powder.

Table 45. Codex Alimentarius Proposed Standards 1971 (minimum amounts/100 g)

Nutrient	Minimum requirement
Protein (g)	1.8
Fat (% of total energy content)	25
Linoleate (mg)	300
Vitamin A (μg)	75 (retinal), 450 (β-carotene)
Vitamin D (IU) (μg)	40 1
Vitamin E (mg)	0.3
Vitamin B_1 (μg)	25
Vitamin B_2 (μg)	60
Vitamin B_6 (μg)	50
Pantothenic acid (μg)	300
Vitamin B_{12} (μg)	0.15
Calcium (mg)	50

Magnesium (mg)	6
Phosphorus (mg)	25
Iron (mg)	1
Iodine (μg)	5

Source: Bender, 1973.

Table 46. Nutritional specifications for Bal-Ahar.

Nutrient	Requirement
Protein	25 ± 4%
PER	> 2.0
Vitamin A	Not less than 1300 units/100g
Fat	2 to 6 %
Fatty acids	Less than 0.02%
Vitamin B_1	Not less than 0.3 mg/100g
Vitamin B_2	Not less than 0.4 mg/100g
Niacin	Not less than 5 mg/100g
Total ash	Not less than 0.5%
Moisture	Maximum 10%
Crude fiber	Maximum 5%
Iron	Not less than 10 mg/100g
Calcium	Not less than 400 mg/100g

Source: Schrimshaw, 1974.

Chapter 17

Snack and Baked Foods

Deep fried foods are very popular in India in rural as well as urban sector. They have longer shelf life. Normally rice is the chief ingredient in the snack foods. Dehulled sorghum flour can be partly substitute in snack foods. Dehulled sorghum and maize can be flaked. In this process sorghum grains are pearled in a polishing machine. This pearled sorghum is wetted, steamed under pressure and then flaked in roller flakers. The flake thus prepared makes an excellent snack food.

Chapter **18**

Dehydrated Foods from Sorghum

18. Dehydrated foods from sorghum:

Usually *papads* are prepared with cereal and pulse combination. But *papads* can be prepared from dehulled sorghum flour (Figure 8).

Dehulled sorghum flour (25 g)

↓

Add chilli powder (7.5 g), salt (12.5g), cumin seeds (5g) and mix well

↓

Add lemon juice (1 tsp)

↓

Add the mixture to boiling water (500 ml) and cook for 10-15 min

↓

Remove from fire and knead well

↓

Make into small round balls

↓

Roll into *papads*

↓

Dry under sun or in dryer

↓

Papads

↓

Store in polythene bags

Figure 8. Processes for preparation of sorghum papads.

Chapter 19

Sorgos for Syrup and Sugar

The juicy, sweet-steamed sorgos have been used in sorghum growing countries for syrup and sugar production on laboratory scale. In this category 100 kg of stalks would yield 50 - 60 kg of juice. While preparation of sugar syrup the boiling should be stopped at 104 ^{0}C. Boiling stop at the temperature of 108 ^{0}C was reached. At this stage it would have a ^{0}Brix reading of 76 - 78^0.

Chapter 20

Sorghum Grain for Livestock Feed

For ruminants: Digestibility of sorghum in cattle 74 while for barley is 84, incase of sheep it was 88% for sorghum and 77% for barley.

Poultry and pigs: The competitive price of mass-produced sorghum has made this an attractive feed grain for pig or poultry producers in the South-Western USA.

Chapter 21

Specific Products from Sorghum

---

1. Sorghum *Hurda* (Sorghum Roasted Grains)

Procedure for the preparation of sorghum *hurda*

First select sorghum earheads of partially mature (soft/milk dough stage) tender stage. Roast the earheads directly on hot fire coke thoroughly. Separate the roasted grains by rubbing on the hard surface when hot. Add salt, lemon juice and chilli powder to taste. Serve it as such when it is hot. It can be preserved in LDPE bag by vacuum packaging for short time. The nutritive value of sorghum *hurda* is given in Table 47.

2. Sorghum cooked Grains (*Ghugarya*)

Ingredient	Quantity
Sorghum grains	250 g
Water	1000 ml
Salt	To taste

Procedure for the preparation of sorghum cooked grains

Take sorghum grains, clean properly and wash it thoroughly. Steep it in hot water for 24 hrs. After that drain it properly. Steam sorghum grains in pressure cooker under 15 Psi for 20 - 25 min. Then remove it from pressure cooker, mix with salt, spices as per requirement and then serve as hot or with any type of curries. The nutritive value of cooked sorghum grains is given in Table 47.

3. Sorghum *Khichadi*

Ingredients	**Quantity**
Pearled sorghum grains	100 g
Rice	25 g
Chickpea dhal	25 g
Groundnuts	50 g
Onion	2
Garlic	6 cloves
Fat	50 g
Mixed spices (mustard, cumin, asafoetida, turmeric)	2 tea spoons
Salt	To taste
Water	As required

Procedure for the preparation of sorghum *Khichadi*

First heat oil in a pot. Add spices and fry onion and garlic. Then add water and boil. When water start boiling add pearled sorghum grains, rice, soaked chickpea, groundnuts and salt. Cover the pot and cook until grains become soft. Serve hot, garnished with grated coconut and green coriander leaves.

4. Sorghum *Pops*

Procedure for the preparation of sorghum *pops*

Pops can be prepared from sorghum grains, but it required special type of sorghum grains (special variety of sorghum), which gives very attractiveness, and fully open *pops*. First clean sorghum grains. Wash it thoroughly. Sprinkle the grains with 2% hot water so as to attain 14 – 16% moisture and cover it for 4 – 6 hrs. Place iron skillet on gas and place salt in the skillet. After sufficient heating place the soaked sorghum grains and allow it to puff for about 5 min. (maximum pop grains). If the popping machine is available the soaked grains can be popped in the machine by adjusting their temperature and moving road distance in the machine. Remove the popped grains by sieving through perforated scoop by separating from salt. As per the requirement mix spices with the popped grains. Serve it when it is hot, it tastes crunchy and crispy. It can be packed immediately into HDPE pouch by vacuum packaging and store for about 6 months. The nutritive value of sorghum *pops* is given in Table 47.

5. Sorghum pop laddu

First prepare sorghum pops as mentioned in the preparation of sorghum pops. The good quality sorghum pops then used for the preparation of sorghum pop laddu.

Ingredient	Quantity
Sorghum pops	1000 g
Jaggary/Sugar	600 g
Water	250 g

Procedure for the preparation of sorghum pop laddu

Dissolve sugar/jaggery in warm water and then heat on medium flame until it get sticky consistency and then add sorghum pops and mix it very well. All pops must be sticky with jaggery/sugar syrup. While it is warm taking small quantity and press with two hands in such a way that it forms a round shape laddu and keep for cooling and hardening. Then pack into plastic bags or plastic container and store in dry clean place. It can remain in good condition for about 15 days.

6. Sorghum pop grits laddu

First prepare sorghum pops as mentioned under preparation of sorghum pops. Then prepare sorghum pops grits using mixer on small scale, for large scale grinding mill can be used.

Ingredient	Quantity
Sorghum pop grits	1000 g
Jaggary/Sugar	600 g
Water	250 g

Procedure for the preparation of sorghum pop grits laddu

Dissolve sugar/jaggery in warm water and then heat on medium flame until it get sticky consistency and then add sorghum pops grits and mix it very well. All pops grits must be sticky with jaggery/sugar syrup. While it is warm taking small quantity and press with two hands in such a way that it forms a round shape laddu and keep for cooling and hardening. Then pack into plastic bags or plastic container and store in dry clean place. It can remain in good condition for about 15 days.

7. Sorghum pop grits *chikki*

First prepare sorghum pops as mentioned under preparation of sorghum pops. Then prepare sorghum pops grits using mixer on small scale, for large scale grinding mill can be used.

Ingredient	**Quantity**
Sorghum pop grits	1000 g
Jaggary/Sugar	600 g
Fat	30 g
Water	250 g

Procedure for the preparation of sorghum pop grits *chikki*

Take water in a frying pan, warm it and then add jaggery/ sugar, heat till it becomes like a soft paste. Add sorghum pop grits, mix well and then transfer the mixture to a greased flat plate and spread evenly. Allow to cool and then cut into attractive pieces. Store in airtight container. It can remain more than 30 days in good condition at room temperature.

8. Sorghum pop flour *chikki*

Prepare sorghum pops as mentioned under sorghum pops preparation. Then grind the sorghum pops into fine powder using grinder/mixer or grinding mill. Then use this sorghum pop flour (80 mesh) for preparation of chikki.

Ingredient	**Quantity**
Sorghum pop flour	1000 g
Jaggary/Sugar	600 g
Fat	30 g
Cardamom powder	1 tea spoon
Water	250 g

Procedure for the preparation of sorghum pop flour *chikki*

Take water in a frying pan, warm it and then add jaggery/ sugar heat till it becomes like a soft paste. Then add sorghum pop flour, cardamom powder, mix well and then transfer the mixture to a greased flat plate and spread evenly. Allow to cool and then cut into attractive pieces. Then store in plastic bags or containers in dry place until use.

9. Sorghum pop flour health drink

First prepare sorghum pops. Then grind sorghum pops in to fine powder using mixer or grinder at home or laboratory scale but for large-scale use grinding mill. Sieve the sorghum pop flour using 80-mesh sieve.

Ingredient	Quantity
Sorghum pop flour	10 g
Badam powder	5 g
Sugar	5 %
Water/Milk	100 ml
Coca powder for flavour	As per requirement

Procedure for the preparation of sorghum pop flour health drink

Ground sugar and badam in to fine powder. Mix it into sorghum pop flour and then add coca powder. This all mixture adds in to warm/cold water or milk and homogenate properly and used as a health drink. It is good health drink for children as well as for adults.

10. Sorghum *Flakes (Pohe)*

Procedure for the preparation of sorghum *Flakes (Pohe)*

First clean and wash the sorghum grains thoroughly. Soak the grains in hot water for about 24 hrs. Drain the water and place sorghum grains in a cooker and steam at 15 Psi for 10 - 15 min. Take it out and pass through flaking machine and dry it under shed. This sorghum flakes/*Poha* can be used in sorghum *Chiwada* preparation or onion-*Poha* preparation. This *Poha* can be preserve by placing in LDPE bags by vacuum packaging. It can be stored upto 2 – 3 months but it is not suitable for storage during winter season. The nutritive value of sorghum Flakes/*Poha* is given in Table 47.

11. Sorghum low fiber flour

Procedure for the preparation of sorghum low fiber flour

Clean sorghum grains properly. Grind it into fine flour using grain-grinding mill. Sieve the flour through 60-mesh sieve and separate coarse material collected on top of the sieve, and then we get low fiber flour. Such type of flour can be used for the preparation of various products. The nutritive value of sorghum low fiber flour is given in Table 47.

12. Sorghum high fiber flour

Procedure for the preparation of sorghum high fiber flour

Clean sorghum grains properly. Grind it into fine flour using grain-grinding mill. Sieve the flour through 80 or 100-mesh sieve and separate small quantity fine flour then we get remaining high fiber flour. Such type of flour can be used for the preparation of specific products. The nutritive value of sorghum high fiber flour is given in Table 47.

13. Sorghum malt flour

Procedure for the preparation of sorghum malt flour

First clean and wash sorghum grains properly. Steep the grains in warm water overnight. Drain water from the grains and wash thoroughly. Place the steeped grains in muslin cloth and tie loosely keeps for the germination at warm place upto 30 - 36 hrs. After germination dry all grains and remove the sprouts and grind into fine flour. Sieve the flour through 60-mesh sieve and separate fine flour and fiber. The fine malted sorghum flour can be used for preparation of various ethnic and health foods. It can be packed in LDPE bags and preserve by vacuum packaging. The nutritive value of sorghum malt flour is given in Table 47.

14. Sorghum diabetic flour

Procedure for the preparation of sorghum malt flour

Take cleaned sorghum grains and grind it into fine flour. Add 20% malt sorghum flour, 5% dehydrated mushroom powder, 2% dehydrated carrot, 5% malted soybean flour, 5% fenugreek leaves powder, 3% bitter gourd powder and 8% malted finger millet whole flour. Sieve mixture of all flours through 20-mesh sieve. Then use such type of flour for preparation of various diabetic foods. This type of flour can be used for the preparation of *Bhakari* or *Thalipeeth*. It can be preserve in LDPE bags by vacuum packaging for short time. The nutritive value of sorghum diabetic flour is given in Table 47.

15. Sorghum *semolina/Rava*

Procedure for the preparation of sorghum *semolina/Rava*

First clean sorghum grains wash it thoroughly. Steep it into hot water for 24 hrs. After that drain the water properly and place the grains in pressure cooker and steam under 15 Psi for 10-15 min. Then remove it from pressure cooker and keep for drying to reduce moisture upto 12%. After that grind sorghum grains in grain Mill coarsely. Sieve it through using 40-mesh sieve to obtain sorghum Semolina/*Rava* grits and flour. Such type of semolina can be used for the preparation of *Idli* or *Dosa*. It can be preserved in LDPE pouch by vacuum packaging and it remains in good condition for about 6 months. The nutritive value of sorghum semolina/*Rava* is given in Table 47.

16. Sorghum *Noodles*

Ingredient	Quantity
Pearled sorghum grain flour	1000 g
Sorghum semolina	250 g
Salt	As per taste
Water	As required to wet the flour

Procedure for the preparation of sorghum *Noodles*

First sieve the sorghum flour and semolina. Then mix with water and knead in to smooth soft dough. After that cook this dough for 5 min in a pressure cooker. Then keep this cooked dough in a pressing machine (*Sorya*) or noodles making machine and press the noodles on a polyethylene paper or sheet. Dry the noodles under sun and then store in the plastic bags for at least 6 months without any disorder. The nutritive value of the sorghum noodles is given in the Table 47.

17. *Kheer* from sorghum *noodles*

Ingredient	Quantity
Sorghum noodles	500 g
Cashew nuts	200 g
Milk	2.5 Liters
Raisins	50 g
Sugar	500 g
Fat	50 g
Salt	To taste
Elachi	10 No
Water	As per requirement

Procedure for the preparation of sorghum *Noodle Kheer*

First fry the noodles with fat on oven separately. Then fry dry fruits with fat in a pan. After that boil the water and milk together then add fried noodles. Cook for some time and then add sugar, mix slowly and cook for 10 – 15 min. At the last add elachi powder and decorate with cashew nuts, raisins and other dry fruits. Serve when it is hot. The nutritive value of the sorghum *noodle kheer* is given in the Table 47.

18. Sorghum *Modak*

Ingredient	Quantity
Sorghum *Semolina/Rava*	200 g
Sorghum flour	200 g
Sugar	100 g
Fat	50 g
Salt	To taste
Water	As per requirement

Procedure for the preparation of sorghum *Modak*

First clean the sorghum *semolina/rava*. Boil the water in a container and add *rava* slowly and cook for few minutes. Then add sorghum flour, sugar, salt and fat in it while mixing simultaneously. When half cooked remove from the flame and cool it, make round balls and then cook like normal *modak* in a pressure cooker or on sieve on hot water container for 10 - 15 min. Cool the modak at room temperature and then serve it as a sweet product. This product can be prepared without sugar and it can serve with tomato/tamarind soup or samber/curry. The nutritive value of the sorghum *modak* is given in the Table 47.

Chapter **22**

Traditional and Ethnic Sorghum Products

1. Sorghum *Dashmi*

Ingredient	Quantity
Sorghum flour	120 g
Wheat flour	80g
Sugar	40 g
Fat/Oil	30 g
Salt	As per taste
Cardamom	6 g
Milk	200 g

Procedure for the preparation of sorghum *Dashmi*

Sorghum and wheat flour sieve together. Add sugar, salt, cardamom powder in milk stir well. Add milk in sorghum and wheat flour, mix well and knead into smooth dough by adding little oil. After that make small ball and spread it like chapatti in round shape. Roast on pre heated iron sheet/Tawa. Apply small quantity of oil on it and roast till it become light brown. Serve it immediately as hot or preserve in airtight LDPE bag for further use. The nutritive value of sorghum *Dashmi* is given in Table 47.

2. Sorghum *Khakara*

Ingredient	Quantity
Sorghum flour	100 g
Wheat flour	If required small quantity
Oil	As per requirement
Salt	As per taste
Turmeric powder	Pinch
Chilli powder	To taste
Water	As per requirement

Procedure for the preparation of sorghum *khakara*

Take sieved sorghum flour, for stickiness adds small quantity of wheat flour. Mix other all ingredients and make dough. Roll it into very thin sheet. Some times this thin sheet can be cut into small strips using a knife. Then shallow fry, till it become brown and crunchy. Such type of product can be stored for at least one week in good condition at room temperature. The nutritive value of sorghum *Khakara* is given in Table 47.

3. Sorghum *Thalipeeth*

Ingredient	Quantity
Plain or malted or *hurda* sorghum flour	150 g
Soybean flour	50 g
Salt	as per taste
Oil	40 ml
Onion (chopped)	100 g
Green chilli (chopped)	to taste
Coriander leaves	20 g
Garlic	to taste
Ginger	to taste
Water	as per requirement

Procedure for the preparation of sorghum *Thalipeeth*

Sieve all flours with sorghum flour using 60-mesh sieve. Cut onion, green chilli, coriander leaves, garlic, ginger in to fine pieces. Make garlic, ginger and chilli paste. Mix sorghum flour and other remaining all ingredients together. Make soft dough with required quantity of water and knead into smooth dough. Take small quantity of dough, make small ball and spread it in a round shape with the help of hand on cloth or polythene paper into round shape. After that place on shallow fry pan or pre-heated Tawa and bake on both sides by applying little oil on it. Serve it as hot with chutney or curd. It can remain in good condition upto one day at room temperature. The nutritive value of sorghum *Thalipeeth* is given in Table 47.

4. Sorghum *papad*

Papad is a snack food item and it is very tasty so it is used in every Indian's diet sine old day. People like this item very much so it has great demand in every corner of the country. A variety of *papads* are prepared from pulses *dhals* and cereals. Basically papads are prepared from black gram dhal, *mung dhal* etc. In South India, *papads* are familiar as *applams*, whereas in Gujarat and Rajasthan as *Khachche*. *Papads* are traditionally prepared by hand rolling methods employing ladies at every house. Papad is a small flat *Chapati* like structure made from *dhal* flour which is kneaded into a stiff dough after mixing with spices, salt, oil and leavening agents. Further, small uniform dough balls are prepared and rolled into flat shape like *chapati* into round shape by hand rolling. Then they are dried upto desirable moisture level and packed into LDPE bags. *Papads* can be classified on the basis of their size and shape as well as ingredients contents in it. Now a days *papads* are produced by using *papad* machines. The malted sorghum flour with malted *ragi* flour produce excellent nutritious papads, having high fiber. Sorghum with other pulses and cereals produce nutritionally superior *papads* than the traditional *papads*. The general procedure of malting of grains is given in Figure 9.

Sorghum / Ragi /Bajara

↓

Grains

↓

Cleaning and washing

↓

Steeping in hot water (overnight)

↓

Drain water and wash thoroughly

↓

Keep in cloth for germination (40 –48 hrs)

↓

Dry at low temperature

↓

Remove germs

↓

Grind into fine flour

↓

Sieving (60-mesh sieve)

↓

Fine malted flour

↓

Use for various types of products

Figure 9. Flow sheet for preparation of malted flour from various crop grains.

A. Malted sorghum *papad*

Ingredient	Quantity
Malted sorghum flour	500 g
Papadkhar	5 g
Salt	20 g
Gingelly seed	5 g
Asafoetida	2.5 g
Cumin seed powder	5 g
Black pepper powder	2.5 g
Water	500 ml

B. High fiber mixed *papad*

Ingredient	Quantity
Malted sorghum flour	375 g
Malted *Ragi* bran	125 g
Papadkhar	5 g
Salt	20 g
Sesamum	5 g
Asafoetida	2.5 g
Cumin seed powder	5 g
Black pepper powder	2.5 g
Ajwan	2.5 g
Water	500 ml

C. Malted mixed sorghum *papad*

Ingredient	Quantity
Malted sorghum flour	500 g
Malted *Ragi* flour	500 g
Papadkhar	10 g
Salt	36 g
Gingelly seed	10 g
Asafoetida	2.5 g
Cumin seed powder	5 g
Black pepper powder	5 g
Water	1000 ml

D. Chilli *papad*

Ingredient	Quantity
Malted sorghum flour	150 g
Malted *Ragi* bran	100 g
Papadkhar	3 g
Salt	12 g
Chilli powder	3 g
Garlic paste	5 g
Gingelly seed	5 g
Asafoetida	2.5 g
Cumin seed powder	5 g
Black pepper powder	2.5 g
Water	450 ml

Procedure for the preparation of all types sorghum *papads*

First sieve all flours together. Boil water and add *papadkhar*, salt, sesame seeds, asafoetida, cumin powder and black pepper powder and all other spices. Then add flour mixture in boiling water, stir well and mix into smooth dough. Divide the dough into small portions 10 – 12 g each ball. Steam the balls in steamer or pressure cooker at 15 Psi for 10 – 15 min. Place the balls in *papad* press machine after enclosing in plastic sheet and press into 0.10 or 0.15 cm thick sheet. Dry at room temperature mostly under shed until get desired moisture. Pack in laminated bags and store at room temperature. It can remain in good condition upto one year without any spoilage. The nutritive value of sorghum *papads* is given in Table 47.

5. Sorghum *Upama*

Upama is generally used as breakfast food and some time as a snack food too. *Upama* mostly prepared using wheat semolina and black gram dhal. But we can prepare *Upama* using sorghum semolina also.

Ingredient	Quantity
Sorghum semolina (*Rava*)	100 g
Groundnut	10 g
Black gram	25 g
Salt	To taste
Sugar	To taste
Green chilli (chopped)	1.5 g
Turmeric powder	1.5 g
Cumin seed	1.5 g
Mustard seed	1.5 g
Asafoetida	2.5 g
Coriander leaves	Few
Curry leaves	Few
Oil	20 ml
Onion (chopped)	50 g
Water	As per requirement

Procedure for the preparation of all types sorghum *Upama*

Sieve sorghum semolina and roast it, till it becomes light brown. Soak black gram dhal in hot water for 8 - 10 min. Cut onion, chilli, coriander leaves, curry leaves. Place deep fry pan on gas and add oil heat for to warm, add mustard, cumin seed, asafoetida, green chilli, curry leaves, groundnut, onion, black gram dhal, turmeric and fry thoroughly and after that add sufficient water in it, boil it and add sorghum semolina, sugar, salt etc. After cooking spread coriander leaves on it and serve as hot by garnishing with coconut shreds and lime piece. The nutritive value of sorghum *Upama* is given in Table 47.

6. Sorghum *Pakoda* (*Bhagi*)

Ingredient	Quantity
Sorghum flour	200 g
Chickpea flour	100 g
Ginger paste	1 tea spoon
Salt	To taste
Chilli powder	To taste
Onion (chopped)	2

Turmeric powder	1 pinch
Green chillies (chopped)	4
Coriander leaves	1 bunch
Curry leaves	1 bunch
Oil	400 ml
Water	As per requirement

Procedure for the preparation of all types sorghum *Pakoda* (*Bhagi*)

Sieve sorghum flour and chickpea flour together. Add salt, chilli powder, chopped onion, chopped green chillies, chopped coriander leaves, ginger paste to the sieved flour and mix with hot water and make smooth dough consistency. Heat the oil and put this dough in different shapes, deep fry using medium flame till it attains golden colour. Serve hot with tomato sauce. The nutritive value of sorghum *Pakoda (Bhagi)* is given in Table 47.

7. Sorghum *Shira* (sweets)

Shira is a sweet product generally used during breakfast. This product is rich in protein, fat and minerals. This product also used for snack to the guests and relatives while visiting as well as to the patients to get more energy.

Ingredient	Quantity
Sorghum semolina (*Rava*)	100 g
Groundnut/Cashew nuts/Raisins	50 g
Sugar	100 g
Elichi fruits	5 g
Salt	To taste
Milk	100 ml
Fat	50 g
Keshari colour	1 pinch
Water	As per requirement

Procedure for the preparation of all types sorghum *Shira* (sweets)

Sieve sorghum semolina and roast it, till it becomes light brown. Place deep fry pan on gas and add oil heat for to warm, add sufficient milk and water in it, boil it and add sorghum semolina, sugar, salt etc. After cooking spread chew nuts/groundnuts/raisins etc. and serve it while hot. The nutritive value of sorghum *Shira* (sweets) is given in Table 47.

8. Sorghum *Rava Idali*

Ingredient	Quantity
Parboiled sorghum semolina (*Rava*)	100 g
Rice	50 g
Salt	To taste
Black gram	50 g
Curd	200 g
Coriander	10 g
Water	As per requirement

Procedure for the preparation of all types sorghum *Rava Idali*

First soak rice and paste it, simultaneously soak the black gram dhal for 8 hrs and drain out the water grind into fine paste. Mix these pastes and ferment overnight. Soak parboiled *Rava* for 1.5 hrs. Add salt, soaked Rava in fermented paste and mix it thoroughly with curd and coriander leaves. Apply teaspoon oil to the *idli* mould and pour *idli* batter in it. Steam it in *idli* cooker for 10 –15 mins, take out and remove *idli* from the moulds and serve hot with chutney. The nutritive value of sorghum *Idali* is given in Table 47.

9. Sorghum *dosa*

Ingredient	Quantity
Sorghum semolina (*Rava*)	80 g
Rice	100 g
Salt	To taste
Black gram	70 g
Oil	200 g
Curd	50 g
Coriander leaves	Few
Colour	As per requirement
Water	As per requirement

Procedure for the preparation of all types sorghum *dosa*

First soak rice and black gram dhal for 8 hrs and drain out the water grind into fine paste. Ferment the batter overnight. Soak parboiled *Rava* for 0.5 hrs. and add salt, soaked *Rava* in fermented paste and mix it thoroughly with curd and coriander leaves. Apply teaspoon oil on the pre heated *Dosa* making *Tawa* and pour dosa batter on it, smear it by round scoop into thin-round shape. Fry it in shallow fry pan/*Tawa* and serve as hot with chutney. The nutritive value of sorghum *dosa* is given in Table 47.

10. Sorghum *Uttappa*

Ingredient	Quantity
Parboiled/plain sorghum semolina (*Rava*)/ Flour	80 g
Rice	100 g
Salt	To taste
Black gram	70 g
Oil	150 g
Onion	200 g
Tomato	200 g
Green chilli	20 g
Coriander leaves	10 g
Water	As per requirement

Procedure for the preparation of all types sorghum *Uttappa*

First soak rice and black gram dhal for 8 hrs and drain out the water, grind into fine paste and add sorghum *Rava* in it. Ferment the batter overnight. Mix it and make it into thin batter consistency by adding required quantity of water. Cut onion, green chilli, coriander leaves, tomato and add in fermented batter. Add salt, and mix well. Put little oil on dosa pan, pour the batter on it and spread the batter round and shallow fry. Serve as hot with chutney or any type of curry. The nutritive value of sorghum *Uttappa* is given in Table 47.

11. Sorghum *Appe*

Ingredient	Quantity
Malted sorghum semolina (*Rava*)	100 g
Rice	50 g
Salt	To taste
Black gram dhal	100 g
Oil	20 g
Cumin seed powder	2 g
Curd	200 ml
Water	As per requirement

Procedure for the preparation of all types sorghum *Appe*

First soak rice and black gram dhal for 6 hrs and drain out the water, grind into fine paste and Ferment overnight. Soak sorghum *Rava* for 0.5 hr mix with curd, sorghum *Rava*, salt, and cumin seed powder into fermented the batter. Apply little oil on *Appe* stand and pour the batter in it. Steam for 10 min. Remove from the Appe stand and serve as hot with chutney. The nutritive value of sorghum *Appe* is given in Table 47.

12. Sorghum *Chiwada*

Ingredient	Quantity
Sorghum flakes	100 g
Groundnut	15 g
Coconut (desiccated/cut)	10 g
Salt	To taste
Oil	10 g
Sugar powder	To taste
Chilli powder	To taste
Turmeric powder	1 Pinch
Cumin seed	2 g
Mustard seed	2 g
Coriander leaves	10 g
Curry leaves	Few
Chew nuts	10 g
Raisins	10 g

Procedure for the preparation of all types sorghum *Chiwada*

Fry sorghum flakes in sufficient quantity of oil. Fry coconut and groundnut. Cut coriander leaves. Add all ingredients in oil and fry well. Add fried flakes in it and mix well. Serve hot or preserve by packing into LDPE bags. For longer storage apply nitrogen gas flush and then seal the pouch. The nutritive value of sorghum *Chiwada* is given in Table 47.

13. Sorghum *Rava laddu*

Ingredient	Quantity
Sorghum *Rava* (semolina)	100 g
Soybean flour	50 g
Sugar powder	40 g
Salt	To taste
Fat	30 g
Almond	8 g
Raisins	8 g
Chew nuts	8 g
Cardamom	1 pinch

Procedure for the preparation of all types sorghum *Rava laddu*

Fry sieved sorghum *Rava* and soybean flour together. Roast the mixture adding fat till it get good smell and light brown colour. Roast chew nuts, almond and raisins in little fat. Add sugar powder chew nuts, almonds, raisins and cardamom powder, in the roasted material and mix it well. Divide the mixture into small equal portions and prepare *laddu*. Serve or store for few days in plastic bags or stainless steel container. The nutritive value of sorghum *Rava laddu* is given in Table 47.

14. Sorghum *Chakali*

Ingredient	Quantity
Sorghum grains	100 g
Wheat	50 g
Rice	50 g
Salt	To taste
Oil	200 g

Green gram dhal	50 g
Bengal gram dhal	50 g
Black gram dhal	25 g
Soybean	25 g
Gingelly seed	15 g
Cumin seed powder	5 g
Ajwan seed	5 g
Chilli powder	To taste
Boiled water	As per requirement

Procedure for the preparation of all types sorghum *Chakali*

Clean, wash, dry all the grains and pulses separately. Roast all separately, mix and grind into fine flour. Sieve flour and add chilli powder, cumin and ajwan seed powder, gingelly seed, salt and boiled oil and mix well into smooth dough. Add boiled water and make smooth dough. Place it into *Chakali* making *Sorya,* press it and put into hot oil for frying. Deep fry in oil using low flame, till it attains golden yellow colour. Serve after cooling and store in plastic bags or in stainless steel container for few days. The nutritive value of sorghum *Chakali* is given in Table 47.

15. Sorghum *Shev*

Ingredient	Quantity
Sorghum flour/malted sorghum flour	100 g
Wheat flour	20 g
Soybean flour	20 g
Cumin seed powder	5 g
Ajwan seed powder	5 g
Chilli powder	10 g
Oil	250 ml
Salt	To taste
Boiled water	As per requirement

Procedure for the preparation of sorghum *Shev*

Mix all flours and then sieve. Then add chilli powder, cumin and ajwan seed powder, salt and small quantity of oil and mix well. Add boiled water and make smooth dough. Place it in shev maker (Sorya) press it in to deep frying oil using low flame, till it attains golden colour.

16. Sorghum *Kurdai*

Ingredient	Quantity
Sorghum grains	1000 g
Salt	To taste
Water	As per requirement

Procedure for the preparation of all types sorghum *Kurdai*

First clean and wash sorghum grains properly. Deep sorghum seeds in excess water for 3 days. Change water everyday. After that wash thoroughly and grind in mixer. Make fine paste. Strain the paste by sieve or muslin cloth. Keep the strained solution aside for one night to settle slurry. After 12 - 15 hrs, remove all water from slurry. Take that slurry and add in sufficient boiling water. After that add salt to taste in it and cook it for 5 –10 min. till to becomes semi- solid or thick slurry. Put it in *Kurdai* press machine/*Sory* and make *Kurdai* into round shape threads. Dry it in sunlight sufficiently. When we want to use it fry in boiling oil. For future use store it in clean container at room temperature. It can remain in good condition upto one year. The nutritive value of sorghum *Kurdai* is given in Table 47.

17. Sorghum *Papadi*

Ingredient	Quantity
Sorghum grains	1000 g
Crushed cumin seed	5 g
Salt	To taste
Colour	As per requirement
Water	As per requirement

Procedure for the preparation of all types sorghum *Papadi*

First clean and wash sorghum grains properly. Deep sorghum seeds in excess water for 3 days. Change water everyday. After that wash thoroughly and grind in mixer. Make fine paste/

slurry. Strain the paste by sieve or muslin cloth. Keep the strained solution aside for one night to settle slurry. After 12 - 15 hrs, remove all water from slurry. Take that slurry and add salt, crushed cumin seed in it and mix it well. Put one tablespoon of batter on a plain plate and rotate it till we get round shape of batter/ *Papadi*. Put this plate for steaming on boiling water for 3 - 5 min. Remove *Papadi* with the help of needle and dry sufficiently under shed. Another way prepare mooth dough of sorghum flour by addition small quantity of chickpea flour, turmeric powder, salt, etc. Then put dough into papadi machine (sory) and press it to give papadi shape product. This product immediately or directly pour into boiling oil to get fried papadi. Serve after frying gives crunchy-n-tasty. The nutritive value of sorghum *Papadi* is given in Table 47.

18. Sorghum *Vada*

Ingredient	Quantity
Sorghum grains	1000 g
Cumin seed powder	5 g
Salt	To taste
Chilli powder	To taste
Water	As per requirement

Procedure for the preparation of sorghum *Vada*

First clean and wash sorghum grains properly. Deep sorghum seeds in excess water for 3 days. Change water everyday. After that wash thoroughly and grind in mixer. Make fine paste/ slurry. Strain the paste by sieve or muslin cloth. Keep the strained solution aside for one night to settle slurry. After 12 - 15 hrs, remove all water from slurry. Take that slurry and add cumin seed powder and salt in it, cook for 5 - 10 min. till it becomes solid. Make small balls and dry it in sunlight sufficiently. Serve after frying in oil. The nutritive value of sorghum *Vada* is given in Table 47.

19. Sorghum Health drink

Ingredients	Quantity
Sorghum grains	3 kg
Ragi grains	1 kg
Soybean	1 kg
Green gram	1 kg
Bajra	2 kg
Arecanuts	300 g
Sugar	150 g
Cocoa powder	As required (for flavour)
Preservative	1 g
Water	As per requirement

Procedure for preparation of health drink

First soak different types of grains in different containers for over night. Then wash the grain with tap water and pack loosely in cloth bags, which are already wetted with, distill water and kept for germination. It may take 2 - 3 days to germinate. These germinated grains are dried in sunlight for 2-3 days. Remove the sprouts then floured finely and separately. Ground the sugar and arecanuts. Mix all different flours and add this sugar mixture to the above flour mixture and add cocoa powder for taste and add preservative to preserve the flour. Add this mixture may be 10 to 15% in warm water or in warm milk and use as a health drink. It is very good health drink for children and also for adults too.

Chapter 23

Bakery Products from Sorghum

Sorghum sweets, biscuits and cookies

Biscuits, sweets and cookies are the most popular common snack food items used by every body at any time. It provides better energy, proteins, minerals and vitamins with longer shelf life. It can be used for incorporating higher amount of proteins, minerals and vitamins. Malted or germinated sorghum can be use for the improvement the nutritional quality of biscuits and cookies. Malting or germination already reported for the improvement in the overall nutritional quality, digestibility of proteins and starch. The higher proportion of dietary fiber of sorghum confers many advantages such as nutritional, digestive and physiological benefits. The high fiber sorghum cookies can provide low calories with high fiber and more resistant starch, which are reported to highly useful for diabetic and obese patients. Malted sorghum flour has been reported to improve the nutritional value. The malted cookies could be specially developed for specific targeted population such as school children, diabetics, and obese people.

1. Sorghum sweet rolls

Ingredient	Quantity
Sorghum flour	400 g
Maida	100 g
Sugar/Jaggery	400 g
Milk	1000 ml
Elachi	5 Nos
Water	As required

Procedure for the preparation of Sorghum sweet rolls

First sieve the sorghum and wheat flours together. Mix these flours with warm water to make dough. Cook this dough in a pressure cooker for 10 min. Grate the jaggery, add some water and boil to dissolve in water. Remove from the flame. Boil the milk, put the dough in to the *sorya* or pressing machine and press it in hot milk step by step by keeping some time gap. Cook for some time and remove from the flame, cool it and mix it in cooled jaggery. Then add elachi powder, cashew nuts and dry fruits for the taste. The nutritive value of the sorghum sweet rolls is presented in Table 47.

2. Sorghum *muffins*

Ingredient	Quantity
Sorghum flour	200 g
Fat	100 g
Sugar powder	150 g
Eggs	4 Nos
Baking powder	3 g
Vanilla	2-3 drops
Sultanas	85 g

Procedure for the preparation of Sorghum *muffins*

First sieve the sorghum flour and baking powder together. Cream the fat and sugar together to get good forth. Beat the eggs thoroughly and mix few drops of essence. Then add beaten eggs to the rubbed fat and sugar mixture. Cut the sultanas and mix to the flour. Add this flour to the above mixture make small balls and bake at 180 °C for 15 –20 minutes in an oven. This can be served as a snack food. The nutritive value of sorghum muffins is given in Table 47.

3. Sorghum *Burffi*

Ingredient	Quantity
Pearled sorghum flour	200 g
Fat	20 g
Sugar	150 g

Groundnuts	50 g
Cashew nuts/Almonds	50 g
Elachi	3 Nos
Colour (yellow/kesari)	As required
Water	As per requirement

Procedure for the preparation of Sorghum *burffi*

Sieve the sorghum flour and then fry in fat or oil. Roast the groundnuts, remove the outer skin and powder it. Make small pieces of all dry fruits. Add water to the sugar and mix and boil to get thread consistency. Remove from the flame and mix the sorghum flour, groundnut flour, and elachi powder and mix well. Grease the tray and spread it all over the tray. Cut this with a knife in diamond or various shape. Serve it as a traditional or occasional sweet. The nutritive value of *burffi* is given in Table 47.

4. Sorghum Cookies

Ingredient	Quantity
Sorghum flour	250 g
Maida	250 g
Sugar powder	280 g
Fat	200 g
Salt	5 g
Dextrose solution	50 ml
Cardamom powder	5 g
Nutmeg powder	5 g
Ammonium bicarbonate	2 g
Sodium bicarbonate	5 g
Water	50 ml

Procedure for the preparation of Sorghum Cookies

First sieve sorghum flour, maida, ammonium bicarbonate, sodium bicarbonate, cardamom powder and nutmeg powder together. Then cream the fat and sugar till gets light and fluffy. Take water and salt make solution and add it in the creamed fat. Add dextrose solution and then sieved flour. Knead the mixture very well and keep for 15 min. After that roll the dough into 0.5 cm thick sheet and cut with fancy biscuit/cookies cutter. Place the cookies/biscuits on baking tray and bake at 180 °C for about 10 - 15 min. to get good colour then remove from the oven, cool it and pack in plastic bags for storage. Such types of biscuits/cookies can remain in good condition upto 10 – 15 days. The nutritive value of such type of cookies and biscuits are given in Table 47.

5. Sorghum orange biscuits

Ingredient	Quantity
Malted sorghum flour	620 g
Malted soybean flour	80 g
Maida	100 g
Sugar powder	450 g
Fat	150 g
Salt	5 g
Orange juice	25 ml
Liquid glucose	50 g
Curd	100 ml
Milk powder	30 g
Orange colour	8 ml
Orange essence	7 ml
Ammonium bicarbonate	3 g
Sodium bicarbonate	5 g

Procedure for the preparation of sorghum orange biscuits

First sieve malted sorghum, soybean flours, maida, milk powder, ammonium bicarbonate, and sodium bicarbonate together. Then cream the fat and sugar till gets light, creamy white and fluffy. Then add flour mixture in it. Take curd, water and salt make solution and add it in the creamed fat. Then add in this orange juice, mix well, and make stiff dough. Add orange colour and orange essence, mix well and stiff dough. Divide the dough into small portions or use rotary moulded biscuit machine/bake at 180 - 190 °C for about 7 - 10 min. to get good colour then remove from the oven, cool it and pack in plastic bags for storage. The nutritive value of such type of cookies and biscuits are given in Table 47.

6. Malted sorghum cookies

Ingredient	Quantity
Malted sorghum flour	400 g
Maida	100 g
Sugar powder	280 g
Fat	200 g
Salt	5 g
Dextrose solution	75 ml
Cardamom powder	5 g
Nutmeg powder	5 g
Ammonium bicarbonate	2 g
Sodium bicarbonate	6 g
Water	35 ml

Procedure for the preparation of malted sorghum Cookies

First sieve malted sorghum flour, maida, ammonium bicarbonate sodium bicarbonate, cardamom powder and nutmeg powder together. Then cream the fat and sugar till gets light and fluffy. Take water and salt make solution and add it in the creamed fat. Add dextrose solution and then malted sieved flour. Knead the mixture very well and keep for 15 min. After that roll the dough into 0.5 cm thick sheet and cut with fancy biscuit/cookies cutter. Place the cookies/biscuits on baking tray and bake at 180 ^{0}C for about 10 - 15 min. to get good colour then remove from the oven, cool it and pack in plastic bags for storage. Such types of biscuits/cookies can remain in good condition upto 10 - 15 days. The nutritive value of such type of cookies and biscuits are given in Table 47.

7. Sorghum chocolate cookies

Ingredient	Quantity
Malted or plain sorghum flour	200 g
Maida	300 g
Sugar powder	280 g
Fat	200 g
Cocoa powder	15 g
Salt	5 g

Dextrose solution	75 ml
Ammonium bicarbonate	2 g
Sodium bicarbonate	6 g
Water	40 ml

Procedure for the preparation of sorghum chocolate cookies

First sieve malted or plain sorghum flour, maida, cocoa powder, ammonium bicarbonate, and sodium bicarbonate together. Then cream the fat and sugar till gets light and fluffy. Take water and salt make solution and add it in the creamed fat. Add dextrose solution and then malted or plain sieved flour. Knead the mixture very well and keep for 15 min. After that roll the dough into 0.5 cm thick sheet and cut with fancy biscuit/cookies cutter. Place the cookies/biscuits on baking tray and bake at 180 ^{0}C for about 10 – 15 min. to get good colour then remove from the oven, cool it and pack in plastic bags for storage. Such types of biscuits/cookies can remain in good condition upto 10 – 15 days. The nutritive value of such type of cookies and biscuits are given in Table 47.

8. Sorghum cookies for diabetic patients

Ingredient	Quantity
Sorghum high fiber flour	400 g
Malted sorghum flour	200 g
Maida	150 g
Malted Ragi bran	50 g
Malted soybean flour	100 g
Fenugreek leaves	150 g
Cumin powder	6 g
Aspartame saccharin	20 g
Fat	250 g
Salt	8 g
Curd	250 g
Bitter gourd	50 g
Dextrose solution	50 ml
Ammonium bicarbonate	3 g
Sodium bicarbonate	6 g
Water	35 ml

Procedure for the preparation of sorghum cookies for diabetic patients

First sieve all flours, maida, ammonium bicarbonate, and sodium bicarbonate together. Then cream the fat and sugar till gets light, creamy white and fluffy. Add cleaned fenugreek leaves paste, bitter gourd paste, cumin seed powder, and then mix well. Take curd, water and salt make solution and add it in the creamed fat. Add dextrose solution and then sieved flour. Knead the mixture very well. After that roll the dough into 0.5 cm thick sheet and cut with fancy biscuit/cookies cutter. Place the cookies/biscuits on baking tray and bake at 180 °C for about 8 - 10 min. to get good colour then remove from the oven, cool it and pack in plastic bags for storage. Such types of biscuits/ cookies can remain in good condition upto 10 - 15 days. The nutritive value of such type of cookies and biscuits are given in Table 47.

9. Sorghum *nankhatai*

Ingredient	Quantity
Malted sorghum flour	300 g
Maida	200 g
Sugar powder	280 g
Cardamom powder	10 g
Fat	150 g
Salt	5 g
Curd	100 g
Dextrose solution	75 ml
Ammonium bicarbonate	2 g
Sodium bicarbonate	5 g

Procedure for the preparation of sorghum *nankhatai*

First sieve malted sorghum flour, maida, cardamom powder, ammonium bicarbonate, and sodium bicarbonate together. Then cream the fat and sugar till gets light, creamy white and fluffy. Take curd, water and salt make solution and add it in the creamed fat. Add dextrose solution and then sieved flour. Knead the mixture very well. Then shape into smooth round ball, place it on greased baking sheets or baking tray and bake at 180 - 190 ^{0}C for about 10 – 15 min. to get good colour then remove from the oven, cool it and pack in plastic bags for storage. Such types of nankhatai can remain in good condition upto 10 – 15 days. The nutritive value of such type of cookies and biscuits are given in Table 47.

10. Sorghum melting moments

Ingredient	Quantity
Malted sorghum flour	55 g
Maida	140 g
Sugar powder	85 g
Butter	115 g
Baking powder	1.5 tea spoon
Egg	1 No
Cashew nut	15 g
Vanilla essence	Few drops
Ammonium bicarbonate	1 g
Sodium bicarbonate	2 g

Procedure for the preparation of sorghum melting moments

Sieve sorghum flour, maida, baking powder, ammonium bicarbonate, and sodium bicarbonate together. Then cream the fat and sugar till gets light, creamy white and fluffy. Add slightly beaten egg and vanilla essence and beat well. Take flour and mix with above mixture and make smooth dough. Divide the dough into small balls and roll in crushed cashew nut and put in a greased and floured baking sheet or tray. Bake in a oven at 180 - 190 ^{0}C for 15 – 20 min, cool and pack in LDPE bags. The nutritive value of such type of cookies and biscuits are given in Table 47.

11. Sorghum peanut cookies

Ingredient	Quantity
Malted or plain sorghum flour	150 g
Maida	350 g
Sugar powder	250 g
Peanut powder	80 g

Butter	200 g
Salt	5 g
Baking powder	1.5 tea spoon
Egg or milk powder	1 No or 10 g

Procedure for the preparation of sorghum peanut cookies

Sieve sorghum flour, maida and baking powder together. Then cream the fat and sugar till gets light, creamy white and fluffy. Add slightly beaten egg and vanilla essence and beat well. Take flour, peanut powder and mix with above mixture and make smooth dough. Add milk if required. Divide the dough into small balls and put in a greased baking sheet or tray. Bake in oven at 180 - 190 ^{0}C for 8 – 10 min, cool and pack in LDPE bags. The nutritive value of such type of cookies and biscuits are given in Table 47.

12. Sorghum masala biscuits

Ingredient	Quantity
Malted or plain sorghum flour	300 g
Maida	300 g
Sugar powder	100 g
Fat	275 g
Green chilli	20 g
Salt	5 g
Curd	150 g
Ammonium bicarbonate	1 g
Sodium bicarbonate	5 g
Ajwan and cumin seed powder	5 g
Coriander leaves	10 g
Dextrose liquid	50 ml

Procedure for the preparation of sorghum masala biscuits

Sieve sorghum flour, maida, chilli powder, anjawan, cumin powder, ammonium carbonate, and sodium carbonate together Then cream the fat and sugar till gets light, creamy white and fluffy. Add curd, dextrose liquid, coriander paste and mix well. Take flour and mix with above mixture and make smooth dough. Add milk if required. Divide the dough into small balls and put in a greased baking sheet or tray. Bake in oven at 180 ^{0}C for 10– 15 min, cool and pack in LDPE bags. The nutritive value of such type of cookies and biscuits are given in Table 47.

13. Sorghum Salt biscuits

Ingredient	Quantity
Malted or plain sorghum flour	400 g
Wheat maida	100 g
Sugar powder	150 g
Fat	200 g
Eggs	2 Nos
Salt	10 g
Baking powder	½ tea spoon
Ammonium bicarbonate	4 g
Water	As required

Procedure for the preparation of sorghum salt biscuits

First sieve sorghum flour, baking powder and maida together. Mix the all flours with fat. Dissolve ammonia bicarbonate, salt, essence and sugar powder in small quantity of water. Add this material to the mixture of flour and fat and make smooth dough with addition of emulsified eggs. Make this dough as a flat 1/8 inch width, and then cut into different shapes using biscuit cutters. Place these biscuits on a greased tray and bake at 170 - 180 ^{0}C temperature for 15 - 20 min in an oven. Cool the salty biscuits and store at room temperature in plastic bags and use when required. Such types of biscuits can remain in good condition for 15 days at room temperature. The nutritive value of sorghum salt biscuits is given in Table 47.

14. Sorghum Sweet biscuits

Ingredient	Quantity
Malted or plain sorghum flour	300 g
Wheat maida	200 g
Sugar powder	300 g
Fat	300 g
Salt	To taste
Baking powder	1 tea spoon
Ammonium bicarbonate	2 g
Essence	Few drops
Water	If required

Procedure for the preparation of sorghum sweet biscuits

First sieve sorghum flour, baking powder, salt, ammonium bicarbonate and maida together. Rub the fat thoroughly and add sugar powder and rub well. Then add few drops of essence and add flour slowly and mix well to a fine dough. Make this dough as a flat 1/8-inch width, and then cut into different shapes using biscuit cutters. Place these biscuits on a greased tray and bake at 170 - 180 °C temperature for 15 - 20 min in an oven. Cool the sweet biscuits and store at room temperature in plastic bags and use when required. Such types of biscuits can remain in good condition for 15 days at room temperature. The nutritive value of sorghum sweet biscuits is given in Table 47.

15. Sorghum Coconut biscuits

Ingredient	Quantity
Malted or plain sorghum flour	500 g
Maida	100 g
Desiccated coconut	200 g
Sugar powder	300 g
Fat	300 g
Salt	To taste
Baking powder	2 tea spoon
Ammonium bicarbonate	4 g
Essence	Few drops
Water	If required

Procedure for the preparation of sorghum coconut biscuits

First sieve sorghum flour, baking powder, ammonium bicarbonate, salt and maida together. Rub the fat thoroughly and add sugar powder and rub well. Then add few drops of essence and add flour slowly with coconut flour and mix well to a fine dough. Make this dough as a flat 1/8-inch width, and then cut into different shapes using biscuit cutters. Place these biscuits on a greased tray and bake at 170 - 180 °C temperature for 15 - 20 min in an oven. Cool the sweet biscuits and store at room temperature in plastic bags and use when required. Such types of biscuits can remain in good condition for 15 days at room temperature. The nutritive value of sorghum coconut biscuits is given in Table 47.

16. Sorghum Peanut biscuits

Ingredient	Quantity
Malted or plain sorghum flour	500 g
Maida	100 g
Peanuts	200 g
Sugar powder	300 g
Fat	300 g
Salt	To taste
Baking powder	2 tea spoon
Ammonium bicarbonate	4 g
Essence	Few drops
Water	If required

Procedure for the preparation of sorghum peanut biscuits

First sieve sorghum flour, baking powder, ammonium bicarbonate, salt and maida together. Cut the peanuts into small pieces and mix with flour. Rub the fat thoroughly and add sugar powder and rub well. Then add few drops of essence and add flour slowly with coconut flour and mix well to a fine dough. Make this dough as a flat 1/8-inch width, and then cut into different shapes using biscuit cutters. Place these biscuits on a greased tray and bake at 170 - 180 ^{0}C temperature for 15 - 20 min in an oven. Cool the peanut biscuits and store at room temperature in plastic bags and use when required. Such types of biscuits can remain in good condition for 15 days at room temperature. The nutritive value of sorghum peanut biscuits is given in Table 47.

The general procedure for the preparation of biscuits and cookies is given in Figure 10.

Sorghum grains + other grains

↓

Cleaning

↓

Processing (malting)

↓

Grind into fine flour

↓

Sieve if necessary

↓

Take coarse/fine flour for formulations

Flours (100%)	Colour (0.01%)
Grind sugar (35%)	Essence (0.1%)
Fat (20%)	Thickening agent
Chemical leavening (0.2%)	Emulsifying, Antioxidants

↓

Water + Milk (30%)

↓

Mix into smooth dough and rest for 30 min.

↓

Roll into sheet (0.5 cm)

↓

Cut into round biscuits or cookies

↓

Bake at 175–190°C for 10–15 min in preheated oven
(till it get brown bake colour)

↓

Cool and pack in airtight container or
in poly pouch after vacuumization

↓

Storage

↓

Marketing

Figure 10. General flow sheet for preparation of sorghum biscuits/ cookies

17. Sorghum *shnkarpale*

Ingredient	Quantity
Sorghum flour	150 g
Maida	300 g
Sugar powder	100 g
Fat	100 g
Salt	3 g
Ammonium bicarbonate	2 g
Baking powder	¼ tea spoon
Cardamom powder	5 g
Dextrose liquid	75 g
Water	35 ml

Procedure for the preparation of sorghum *shnkarpale*

Sieve sorghum flour, maida and baking powder together. Then cream the fat and sugar till gets light, creamy white and fluffy. Add water and cardamom powder. Then mix sieved flour and make smooth dough. Roll the dough into 0.5 cm thickness and cut with knife and make small squares shapes. Fry in oil/fat at 170 ^{0}C for10– 15 min, cool and pack in LDPE bags. The nutritive value of such type of *shnkarpale* is given in Table 47.

18. Sorghum sponge cake

Ingredient	Quantity
Malted or plain sorghum flour	40 g
Maida	75 g
Sugar powder	115 g
Fat	75 g
Salt	1 g
Egg	2 No
Milk powder	20 g
Baking powder	¼ tea spoon
Vanilla essence	Few drops
Water	As required

Procedure for the preparation of sorghum sponge cake

Sieve sorghum flour, maida, milk powder and baking powder together. Then cream the fat and sugar till gets light, creamy white and fluffy. Beat the eggs and beat into cream fat and pour into the sieved flour, add few drops of essence. Add water if required to get a dropping consistency. Pour the mixture into a waxed paper lined cake tin and bake at 175 ^{0}C for 10 – 12 min, cool and pack in LDPE bags. The nutritive value of such type of sponge cake is given in Table 47.

19. Sorghum Fruit cake

Ingredient	Quantity
Malted or plain sorghum flour	150 g
Maida	50 g
Pulpy fruits (pulp)	100 g
Sugar powder	70 g
Fat	75 g
Salt	1 g
Egg	3 No
Milk powder	10 g
Baking powder	¼ tea spoon
Sodium bicarbonate	1 tea spoon
Vanilla essence	Few drops
Milk	As required

Procedure for the preparation of sorghum fruit cake

Sieve sorghum flour, maida, milk powder and baking powder together. Then cream the fat and sugar till gets light, creamy white and fluffy. Beat the eggs and beat into cream fat and pour into the sieved flour, add few drops of essence and pulp of the fruit. Add milk if required to get a dropping consistency. Pour the mixture into a waxed paper lined cake tin and bake at 175 ^{0}C for 10 – 12 min, cool and pack in LDPE bags. The nutritive value of such type of fruitcake is given in Table 47.

Table 47. Nutrients available through various types products prepared from sorghum.

Product	Proteins (%)	Carbo-hydrates (%)	Fat/ Oil (%)	Fiber (%)	Energy (Kcal)	Minerals (%)	Calcium (mg, %)	Iron (mg, %)	Vit. A (µg)
Sorghum flour low fiber	10.50	65.3	3.0	3.2	340	1.2	-	-	-
Sorghum flour high fiber	9.80	66.8	2.8	4.9	320	1.8	-	-	-
Sorghum *pop*	9.50	68.5	2.6	1.8	340	1.6	-	-	-
Sorghum *rava Semolina*	10.40	63.8	3.2	1.6	370	1.6	-	-	-
Sorghum *noodles*	11.3	56.7	1.6	0.8	335	1.2	-	-	-
Sorghum *noodles Kheer*	8.9	23.5	13.5	0.6	260	0.9	-	-	-
Sorghum *Modak*	12.5	60.5	1.8	0.8	330	1.1	-	-	-
Boiled sorghum	9.50	69.3	1.6	1.6	340	1.5	-	-	-
Roasted sorghum (*Hurda*)	8.00	70.2	1.5	1.4	350	1.3	-	-	-
Sorghum flakes	10.40	68.3	1.8	1.6	370	1.2	-	-	-
Sorghum flour for diabetic patients	15.60	61.3	1.9	6.4	435	2.8	-	-	-
Sorghum malt flour	14.50	69.8	2.3	1.5	343	0.8	-	-	-
Sorghum roti / Bhakari	12.64	66.8	2.1	1.8	343	1.8	18	9	-
Sorghum *dashami*	10.30	65.9	2.0	1.4	289	1.4	75	-	-
Malted sorghum flour *thalipeeth*	12.70	69.8	5.6	1.8	394	0.9	108	5	1237

Sorghum *upama*	9.40	56.8	5.7	1.6	326	1.1	61	4	-
Sorghum *Pakoda*	7.5	25.7	53.8	1.3	650	1.2	-	-	-
Sorghum *shira* (sweet)	8.73	58.3	15.6	1.7	432	0.8	32	6	-
Malted sorghum flour *papad*	13.00	69.8	1.6	2.8	354	3.4	43	58	-
High fiber *papad*	12.00	71.3	1.5	3.8	348	2.3	122	60	-
Malted mix *papad*	10.23	69.9	1.9	1.8	345	2.4	203	-	-
Sorghum-chilli papad (Spicy-papad)	10.00	69.5	1.6	1.8	361	1.6	198	-	-
Sorghum *idli*	8.00	65.4	1.8	1.8	200	1.8	103	-	-
Sorghum *dosa*	10.00	63.4	1.9	1.6	593	1.4	31	-	-
Sorghum uttapa	8.00	58.6	6.5	1.6	374	1.3	36	1.2	222,IU
Sorghum appe	10.00	55.8	3.4	1.5	248	1.8	105	3.0	-
Sorghum khakara	10.00	60.3	1.9	1.5	441	1.8	21	3.3	-
Sorghum chiwada	9.33	68.7	1.8	1.5	399	1.3	65	2.3	-
Sorghum-soy ladoo	17.00	65.8	2.5	1.5	648	2.2	98	3.2	-
Sorghum *chakali*	11.20	68.2	18.2	1.4	570	2.0	101	18.0	-
Sorghum *Kurdai*	10.40	40.1	21.5	1.4	349	1.2	25	1.3	-
Sorghum *papadi*	11.00	43.8	23.6	1.5	353	1.2	36	1.6	-
Sorghum masala *vada*	11.00	65.3	20.3	1.5	358	1.6	52	2.3	-
Sorghum *ambil*	13.50	57.6	1.8	1.4	409	1.4	174	65	-
Sorghum cookies	6.00	60.8	5.8	1.4	412	1.1	11	4	-

Malted sorghum cookies	6.00	68.3	1.9	1.5	421	1.1	13.3	3.2	-
Sorghum chocolate cookies	5.20	66.5	9.5	1.6	415	1.2	12.4	2.2	-
Cookies for diabetic patients	12.60	69.8	18.5	6.4	435	1.1	-	-	-
Sorghum *nankhatai* cookies	6.00	58.6	10.0	1.5	370	1.0	25	3.0	-
Sorghum milting moments	7.00	56.9	11.8	1.6	493	1.4	24	-	-
Sorghum *shankarpale*	6.50	58.6	22.3	1.4	381	1.4	17	2	-
Sorghum-groundnut cookies	7.50	42.8	15.3	1.5	464	1.4	21	2.5	565
Sorghum Burffi	8.9	65.3	11.5	0.6	420	1.3	-	-	-
Sorghum Sweet roles	5.6	38.9	3.5	0.8	230	1.2	-	-	-
Sorghum Muffins	15.3	56.3	8.5	1.3	650	1.4	-	-	-
Sorghum Salt biscuits	8.7	41.5	23.3	1.1	422	1.0	-	-	-
Sorghum Sweet biscuits	7.5	57.1	27.3	0.9	510	0.6	-	-	-
Sorghum Coconut biscuits	5.7	40.5	30.3	0.8	430	0.9	-	-	-
Sorghum Peanut biscuits	7.5	65.5	9.3	1.5	465	1.4	21	2.5	560
Sorghum masala biscuits	6.20	63.3	2.9	1.4	407	1.4	33	3	-
Sorghum cake	8.00	60.2	12.6	1.5	418	1.4	88	-	-
Fruits cake	9.6	63.5	11.4	1.4	415	1.2	-	-	-

Chapter **24**

Industrial/Nutraceutical products from sorghum

1. Malting of sorghum for brewing industry

The malting of sorghum reduced the content of starch and increased the reducing sugars. The malting also improved *in vitro* protein digestibility (IVPD) from 80.30 to 83.60 %. The malted cereals and pulses are mostly utilized in the preparation of weaning food (infant food). Malted cereals as well as pulses make all major nutrients easily digestible by hydrolysis process and convert into very simplest form, which can absorb in the digestible system very easily (Table 48).

Table 48. Proximate composition of sorghum and sorghum malt.

Constituent (%)	M 35-1		Swati		CSH 5		PVK-801	
	Grain	Malt	Grain	Malt	Grain	Malt	Grain	Malt
Moisture	10.13	8.13	11.02	8.48	10.83	8.93	10.00	7.91
Crude protein	11.60	11.60	10.70	10.70	11.30	11.30	9.45	9.42
Crude fat	2.93	2.87	2.83	2.78	2.98	2.81	3.00	2.90
Crude fibre	2.13	2.10	2.35	2.10	2.48	2.39	2.10	2.00
Starch	76.23	68.13	77.24	67.83	76.81	66.35	74.20	59.50
Reducing sugar	0.20	1.40	0.10	0.70	0.10	1.40	0.30	0.70
Total minerals	1.70	1.40	1.61	1.43	1.30	1.10	1.20	0.90
Malting losses	-	13.67	-	16.15	-	17.50	-	19.00

Use of sorghum in brewing industry (sorghum beer):

In sole sorghum beer (without adjunct), the bitterness and free amino nitrogen content were low compared to sorghum adjunct beer, which had highest free amino nitrogen content and essential for the beer flavour (Table 49).

Brewing is said to raise the nutritional value of sorghum since it adds Vitamins, neutralizes most of the tannins, hydrolyzes the starch to more digestible forms and increases the availability of minerals and vitamins. South African studies indicate that iron is 12 times more available in sorghum beer than in boiled sorghum gruel, riboflavin may be almost twice and thiamine almost a third more available while niacin's availability remains unchanged (Figure 11).

Enzymes in the malt begin to saccharify the starch. Bacteria then act on a part of the sugar to form lactic acid and some B vitamins. This sweet wort may be drunk after less than one day's fermentation. It contains more B vitamins and negligible amount alcohol. After the first day the mixture is heated and various fungal spores germinate and lead to the production of hydrolytic enzymes. A little millet or sorghum may be specially germinated, then dried as a yeast source. The yeasts multiply and fermentation develops, with the production of alcohol, more B vitamins and new proteins, while the bacteria continue to develop lactic acid. The brew may be drunk after 4-5 days, and in some areas more malted grain may be added to it a day before it is used.

Table 49. Chemical composition of beer from sorghum

Constituent	Malt beer	Adjunct beer
Protein (%)	2.68	1.98
Free amino nitrogen (%)	74.61	119.01
Total sugars (%)	1.54	0.95
Reducing sugars (%)	0.05	0.02
Alcohol (%)	4.66	4.50
Colour (EBC)	5.89	8.58
Specific gravity	1.03	0.98
Bitterness (BU)	6.56	7.58

Sorghum grains

Soaking

↓

Germination

↓

Drying of malted grains

↓

Ground to fine flour

↓

Malted flour

↓

Add cold water to prepare slurry

↓

Add more pounded/steeped sorghum grains in it

↓

Keep for fermentation

↓

Filtration

↓

Bottling of malt beer

↓

Storage

Figure 11. Flowchart for preparation of sorghum beer.

2. Standardization of suitable process for the extraction and recovery of starch from moulded and blackened sorghum grains

The black sorghum grains were soaked in distilled water for 24 hrs to 168 hrs separately at ambient temperature (27 ± 2 ^{0}C) and 60 ^{0}C. The soaking water was changed after every 24 hrs. The soaking grains were blended with water (1:2, w/v) in a laboratory blender for 2 min. The blending was repeated for two more minutes after a pause of 1 min. The slurry was screened through a double-layered muslin cloth. The residue on the muslin cloth was washed with additional water to solubilize and filterate out the remaining starch. The filterate was centrifuged at 8000 x g for 30 min. The supernatants were discarded and the residue was suspended in 0.2 per cent sodium hydroxide solution to solubilize the proteins. The contents were allowed to stand for 3 to 4 hrs to settle the starch. The yellowish upper sodium hydroxide layer was decanted and the settled starch was resuspended in sodium hydroxide until the sodium hydroxide layer became colourless. The settled starch was then washed with water and the contents were screened through the 0.045 mm sieve. The filterate was centrifuged and the starch obtained was recorded as residue in centrifuge tubes and dried at ambient temperature (Figure 12).

A maximum absorption of water was observed in the grins soaked at 60 ^{0}C for 96 hrs. However, the highest starch yield was obtained when the grains were soaked at 60 ^{0}C for 144 hrs. The dilute alkali (0.2%) was found to be superior grain soaking and residue washing medium than the dilute acids or water. A significant higher starch yield was obtained with the use of 0.045 mm sieve (59.3%) as a slurry filtration device as compared to that of muslin cloth (33.8%).

The starch obtained with muslin cloth exhibited slightly higher purity but significantly lower recovery. A soaking of grains for 144 hrs at 60^{0}C in 0.2 per cent NaOH followed by grinding in water and filtration of the slurry through 0.045 mm sieve, centrifugation of the filterate at 8000 x g for 30 min, washing of the residue in 0.2 per cent NaOH followed by water washing, centrifugation and drying of the residue has been standardized to obtain a maximum of 62.2 per cent bright starch from molded and blackened sorghum. The product contained 91.6 per cent starch.

A process to get white starch from the mould-infected sorghum with black or red / brown discoloration is described. It involves soaking of grains in 0.2% solution of H_2SO_4 or NaOH (1:2, w/v) for 12 hrs at 60 °C followed by blending in the same extract for 2-3 min and filtration of slurry through 0.045 mm sieve (Figure 13). The extracted starch is recovered by centrifugation of the filterate at 8000 x g for 20 min, washing the starch-pellet with water to remove residual acid/alkali and drying the product at 40 °C. Sodium hydroxide was suitable for extraction of starch from grains with both black and red / brown discoloration while H_2SO_4 was suitable for only blackened grains. The physico-chemical properties of sorghum starch are given in Table 50 to 59.

Table 50. Water absorption by mould infected blackened sorghum.

Grain soaking temperature °C	Weight gain after soaking of grains (hrs)			
	6	12	24	Mean
30	24.8 + 0.6	31.9 + 0.7	38.7 + 0.8	31.8
40	27.2 + 0.7	33.6 + 0.6	40.1 + 0.4	33.7
50	37.7 + 0.6	36.4 + 0.8	42.6 + 0.7	38.9
60	39.9 + 0.7	42.9 + 0.6	43.0 + 0.4	41.9
70	41.1 + 0.4	43.0 + 0.5	43.1 + 0.6	42.4
Mean	34.1	37.6	41.5	37.7

Table 51. Effect of soaking medium on extraction and recovery of starch from black sorghum.

Grain soaking medium (%)	Extracted starch (%)
NaOH, 0.1	52.00 ± 2.4
H_2SO_4, 0.1	23.38 ± 1.8
Lactic acid, 0.1	34.4 ± 1.9
Water	33.8 ± 2.1

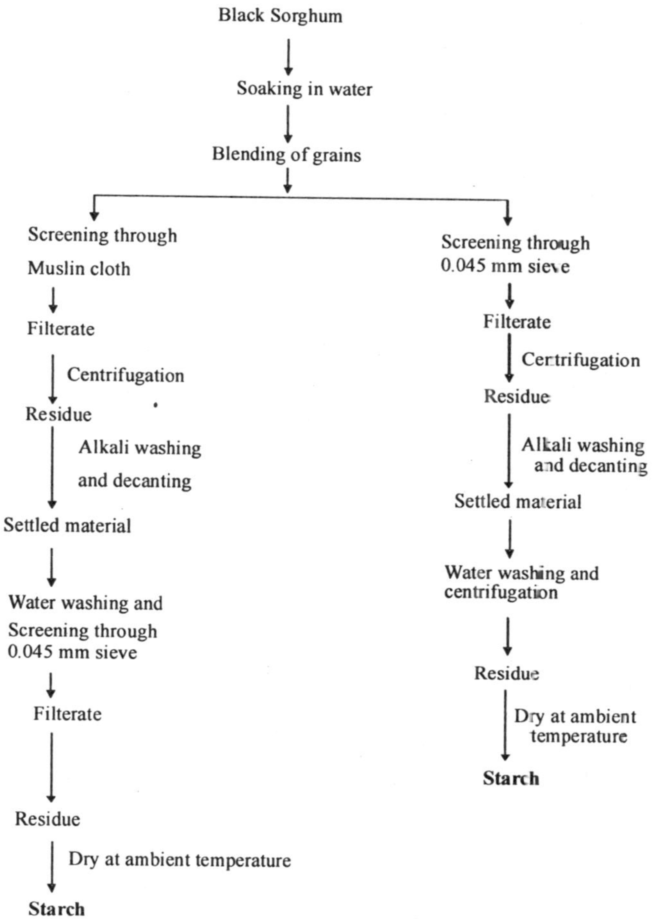

Figure 12. Standardization of starch extraction processes from sorghum.

Table 52. Effect of different soaking periods and extraction media on yield of starch from black sorghum.

Soaking and extraction medium	Starch yield (%) after soaking grains (hrs)		
	6	12	24
Water	45.7 ± 1.6	52.2 ± 1.8	53.0 ± 1.7
Lactic acid, 0.2%	49.4 ± 1.9	56.7 ± 1.5	57.2 ± 1.5
Potassium metabisulphite, 0.2%	50.0 ± 1.8	59.2 ± 1.6	60.0 ± 1.7
Sodium hydroxide, 0.2%	52.8 ± 1.7	64.0 ± 1.4	64.3 ± 1.6
Sulphuric acid, 0.2%	53.7 ± 1.9	63.8 ± 1.8	64.1 ± 1.5

Table 53. Effect of increasing concentration of alkali as soaking medium on starch extraction and recovery.

NaOH concentration (%)	Starch recovery (%)
0.1	52.0 ± 2.4
0.2	54.4 ± 2.6
0.5	54.8 ± 2.8

Table 54. Effect of screening method on recovery of starch.

Screening method	Starch recovery (%)
Muslin cloth	33.8 ± 1.6
Sieve (0.045 mm)	59.3 ± 2.7

Table 55. Effect of period and temperature of soaking of grains on the extraction and recovery of starch from black sorghum grains.

Soaking period (hrs)	Starch recovery (%) at	
	27 ± 2 ^{0}C	60 ^{0}C
24	17.9 ± 0.50	18.4 ± 0.90
48	20.2 ± 1.30	20.8 ± 1.10
72	23.7 ± 0.80	24.7 ± 0.80
96	27.2 ± 1.60	27.6 ± 1.20
120	28.5 ± 0.80	32.1 ± 1.60
144	32.0 ± 0.95	33.8 ± 0.85
168	32.4 ± 0.80	34.0 ± 0.60

Table 56. The yield, content and recovery of starch by different methods of extraction.

Sr. No	Type of method used			Percent starch in black grain	Starch product from grain, %	Actual starch content in extracted product, %	Starch recovery on initial grain basis, %
	SM	BM	RW				
1.	W	W	N	64.7	33.8 ± 1.20	96.0 ± 1.59	50.2 ± 1.60
2.	N	W	N	64.7	52.0 ± 1.80	93.8 ± 1.65	75.4 ± 1.75
3.	N	N	W	64.7	48.3 ± 1.90	94.7 ± 1.57	70.7 ± 1.70
4.	W	W	N	64.7	59.3 ± 1.80	92.0 ± 1.83	84.3 ± 1.81
5.	N	W	N	64.7	62.2 ± 1.95	91.6 ± 1.92	88.0 ± 1.79
6.	N	N	W	64.7	61.8 ± 1.10	92.2 ± 1.50	88.1 ± 1.67

Method 1 to 3 with muslin cloth, Method 4 to 6 with 0.045 mm sieve.
SM = Soaking medium, BM = Blending medium, RW = Residue washing medium
W = Water, N = NaOH (0.2%).

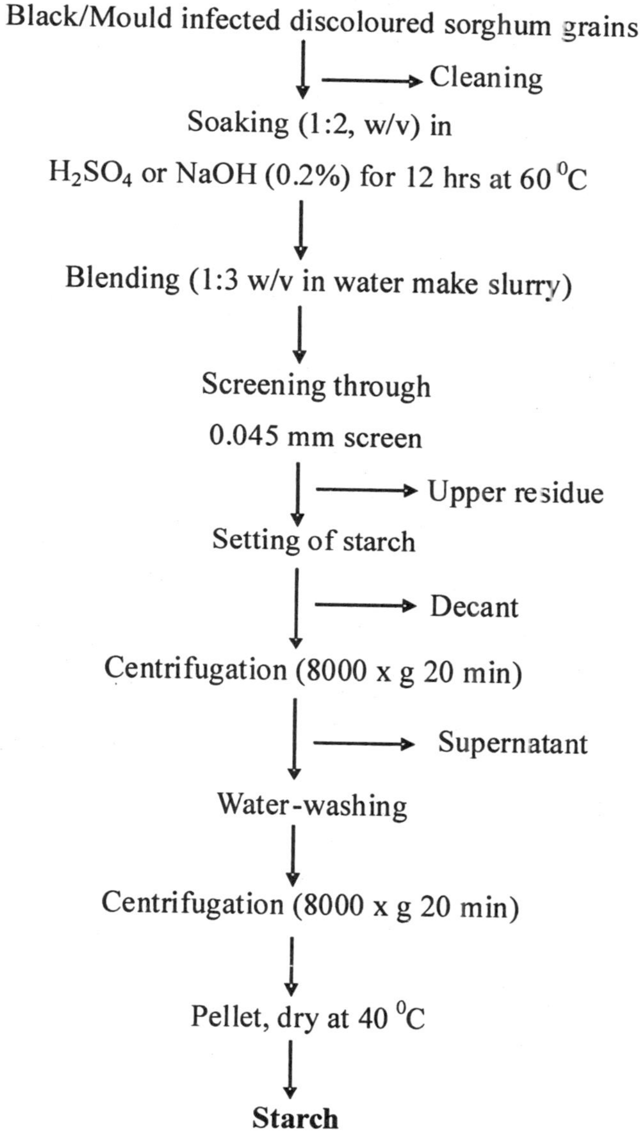

Figure 13. Standardized process for extraction of starch from black/ mould-infected discoloured sorghum grains.

Table 57. Chemical composition of starch extracted by different method.

Starch extraction method	Starch, %	Moisture, %	Protein, %	Total sugars, %	Total ash, %
1.	96.0 ± 1.59	4.5 ± 0.33	0.47 ± 0.10	0.47 ± 0.02	0.50 ± 0.03
2.	93.8 ± 1.65	4.0 ± 0.35	1.03 ± 0.09	0.45 ± 0.01	0.25 ± 0.02
3.	94.7 ± 1.60	5.0 ± 0.29	1.24 ± 0.08	0.43 ± 0.03	0.10 ± 0.04
4.	92.0 ± 1.57	4.5 ± 0.25	1.06 ± 0.06	0.41 ± 0.05	0.39 ± 0.02
5.	91.6 ± 1.92	4.8 ± 0.30	1.23 ± 0.07	0.45 ± 0.04	0.40 ± 0.03
6.	92.2 ± 1.50	4.8 ± 0.25	1.66 ± 0.06	0.43 ± 0.03	0.42 ± 0.01

Method 1 to 3 with muslin cloth, Method 4 to 6 with 0.045 mm sieve.
Methods: 1. WWN, 2. NWN, 3. NNW, 4.WWN, 5. NWN, 6. NNW
SM = Soaking medium, BM = Blending medium, RW = Residue washing medium
W = Water, N = NaOH (0.2%).

Table 58. Functional properties of extracted starch from black sorghum.

Starch extraction method	Water absorption capacity (ml/g)	Oil absorption capacity (ml/g)	Gelatinization temperature (°C)
1.	0.90 ± 0.06	0.99 ± 0.05	78.6 ± 1.2
2.	1.12 ± 0.07	1.18 ± 0.06	77.2 ± 1.1
3.	1.20 ± 0.06	1.11 ± 0.07	78.0 ± 1.01
4.	0.92 ± 0.07	1.32 ± 0.04	80.2 ± 1.10
5.	0.93 ± 0.05	0.99 ± 0.06	76.8 ± 1.30
6.	0.95 ± 0.06	1.01 ± 0.05	78.3 ± 1.15

Method 1 to 3 with muslin cloth, Method 4 to 6 with 0.045 mm sieve.
Methods: 1. WWN, 2. NWN, 3. NNW, 4.WWN, 5. NWN, 6. NNW
SM = Soaking medium, BM = Blending medium, RW = Residue washing medium
W = Water, N = NaOH (0.2%).

Table 59. Physicochemical properties of starch extracted from black or red/brown discoloured sorghum.

Parameter	Whole grains	H_2SO_4 extracted starch	NaOH extracted starch
Moisture, %	9.5	3.4	4.0
Starch, %	67.6	94.5	94.0
Protein, %	9.5	0.7	0.8
Ash, %	1.7	0.3	0.4
Fat. %	2.4	0.9	0.9
Fiber, %	2.2	-	-
GT, ^{0}C	-	77.5	78.3
Colour	Black	White	White
Appearance	Red/brown	Pinkish	White

*GT = Gelatinization temperature.

3. Starch and maltodextrin from sorghum

The starch prepared from black sorghum grain have a vital role and potential raw material for the production of maltodextrin and it may be explored for industrial or commercial exploitation in different food products as fat replacer to reduce the calorific value. Metabolisms of maltodextrins are similar to starch. Food products for diabetic patients can be prepared by using maltodextrins as a fat replacer. Maltodextrins gives hypoglycemic activity and it also a promising food substance to heart patients because it acts as a very good hypocholesterlemic agent.

The maximum amount of maltodextrin was liberated at 4.5% concentration of hydrochloric acid hydrolysis process at 120 minutes interval i.e., 95 per cent and 92 per cent for PVK 801 and CSH 9 sorghum varieties and their dextrose equivalents were 9 and 8 respectively. The maltodextrin contained 98 and 97 per cent total carbohydrate in PVK 801 and CSH 9 respectively (Table 60). The results of reheological attributes particularly the pasting behaviour of maltodextrin revealed that the viscosity at 40 ^{0}C was found to be maximum and then decreased as the temperature increased. The microscopic examination of maltodextrin granules revealed that they are mostly irregular shaped particle aggregates with 4 – 5 μ in size (Table 61). The results indicated that good quality cookies and toffees could be prepared using maltodextrin with 3 per cent replacement of shortening. Maltodextrins are metabolized similar to starch. Thus, fat replacers like maltodextrin can be recommended for use in food products for diabetics, it exhibits hypoglycemic activity. Moreover, it will be a very promising for heart patients also as it acts as a very good hypocholesterlemic agent. The comparative characteristics of starch and maltodextrin of sorghum is given in Table 62 and Figure 14.

Table 60. Chemical composition and physical parameters of sorghum starch.

Parameter	Content (%)	
	PVK-801	**CSH-9**
Moisture	9.80	9.50
Protein	1.10	1.29
Fat	0.90	0.95
Ash	0.24	0.45
Crude fiber	0.73	0.67
Total carbohydrate	96.81	95.60
Yield of starch	75.50	72.85
Granule shape	Polygonal to round	Polygonal to round
Granule size	8.0-9.5 μ	8.0-9.1 μ
Colour of starch	Bright white	Mild white
Iodine affinity	4.4	3.9
Bulk density	0.59	0.58
Molecular weight		
Amylose (daltan)	2,45,000 ± 10,000	2,45,000 ± 10,000
Amylopectin (daltan)	> 0.59 x 10^6	> 0.59 x 10^6

Table 61. Physico-chemical constituents of maltodextrin.

Parameter	Content (%)	
	PVK-801	CSH-9
Moisture	8.0	7.6
Protein	0.05	0.07
Carbohydrate	98.0	97.0
Fat	0.07	0.08
Ash	0.6	0.7
Bulk density	0.579	0.575
Granule shape	Irregular	Irregular
Granule size	3-5 μ	4-5 μ
Granule colour	Bright white	White
Molecular weight		
Amylose (daltan)	1,75,000 $\pm$ 5000	1,75,000 $\pm$ 5000
Amylopectin (daltan)	> 0.59 x 10^6	> 0.59 x 10^6
Dextrose equivalent	9	8

Table 62. Physico-chemical properties of sorghum starch and maltodextrin.

Constituent	Starch	Maltodextrin
Moisture (%)	9.50-9.80	7.5-8.0
Protein (%)	1.10-1.29	0.05-0.07
Fat (%)	0.90-0.95	0.07-0.08
Ash (%)	0.24-0.45	0.6-0.7
Fiber (%)	0.67-0.73	0.4-0.5
Total carbohydrates (%)	95.60-96.81	97-98
Yield (%)	73-76	-
Granule shape	Round, polygonal	Irregular
Granule size (μ)	8.0-9.5	3.0-5.0
Colour of granule	Bright white	Mild white
Iodine affinity	3.9-4.4	-
Bulk density	0.58-0.59	0.57-0.59
Molecular weight of Amylose (daltan)	2,45,000	1,75,000
Molecular weight of Amylopectin (daltan)	> 0.59 x 10^6	> 0.59 x 10^6

Sorghum grains

↓

Cleaning (Removal of foreign matters)

↓

Steeping in water (20 hrs, at 50 °C and 4.5 pH)
(750 ppm KMS, 0.002 M $HgCl_2$, few drops of toluene in water)

↓

Washing with clean water

↓

Blending / preparation of slurry (1:3 w/v, seed : water)

↓

Separation of starch
(Squeezing of slurry through muslin cloth and then passing through 150 µ sieve)

↓

Protein denaturation
(Add 1.5 g NaCl and 5 ml Toluene in slurry)

↓

Shaking for 1 hr

↓

Centrifugation at 4200 RPM for 15 min.

↓

Isolation of starch

↓

Drying (Vacuum drying)

↓

Air drying for overnight

↓

Starch

↓

Acid hydrolysis
(4.5 % HCl conc. 50 °C temp. and 120 min. time)

↓

Isolation —(Vacuum drying)→ Maltodextrin

Figure 14. Flow diagram for the isolation and purification of starch and maltodextrin.

4. Production of high fructose syrup from sorghum starch

The sorghum genotypes cultivated in *kharif* season contain about 68 to 76 per cent starch. The starch is a potential raw material being used in several cloth, paper, dye as well as in food industry in India and foreign country also. Therefore, the production of starch from *kharif* sorghum is one of the most prominent sources because most of the high yielding hybrids mostly cultivated during *kharif* season. For the preparation of value addition products from rain damaged *kharif* season sorghum and also to exploit it for industrial utilization, preparation of starch and its conversion into other valuable products such as high fructose syrup, maltodextrin, sweeteners, carboxymethylated starch, glucose, and sorbitol is most essential.

Fructose is the sweetest sugar among the natural sugars. The relative sweetness of fructose is a function of concentration, temperature and pH, with the maximum sweetness value being found in cooled, dilute solutions that is neutral or slightly acidic. Fructose has a short sweetness duration that tends to enhance the aroma and flavours of fruits. The high fructose syrup can be prepared from sorghum (Plate 12, Figure 15a and 15b) as well as sweetener too (Figure 15c). The refractive index for high fructose syrup (HFS) prepared from CSH 18 starch (1.453) was same as that of HFS from glucose sample (1.455). Colour of the syrup prepared from starch was yellowish and the colour of the HFS prepared from control glucose sample was whitish yellow (Table 63).

Commercially sucrose is usually marketed as sucrose or medium invert sugar, which is liquid and contains 50 parts sucrose, 25 parts dextrose and 25 parts fructose. High fructose sorghum syrup is similar to total sucrose invert; therefore, it replaced sucrose on weight-to-weight basis. Due to the refining to remove non-sweetener components and because of excessive microbiological control, HFS is a very high quality liquid sweetener. The predominant user of HFS is the soft drink industry. The mango squash prepared by using HFSS had recorded higher preference for all the attributes than that of control. The high fructose sorghum syrup can be effectively used to replace sucrose in the products like fruit squashes.

Sorghum starch

← Dextrinization with acid hydrolysis
← Liquification by α-amylase
← Saccharification with Glucoamylase

↓

Glucose syrup (95-96 %) Dextrose

← Refining
← Demineralization
← Decolourisation

↓

Purification

↓

Purified glucose and syrup

↓

Isomerization

← With glucose isomerase
Temperature 60 ^{0}C
pH 6.8-7.0

↓

High fructose sorghum syrup (HFSS)

↓

Purification

← Decolourization using
carbon celite column

↓

HFSS (45 % D.S.)

↓

Evaporation

↓

HFSS (54-55 % D.S.)

Figure 15a. Production of high fructose syrup from sorghum starch

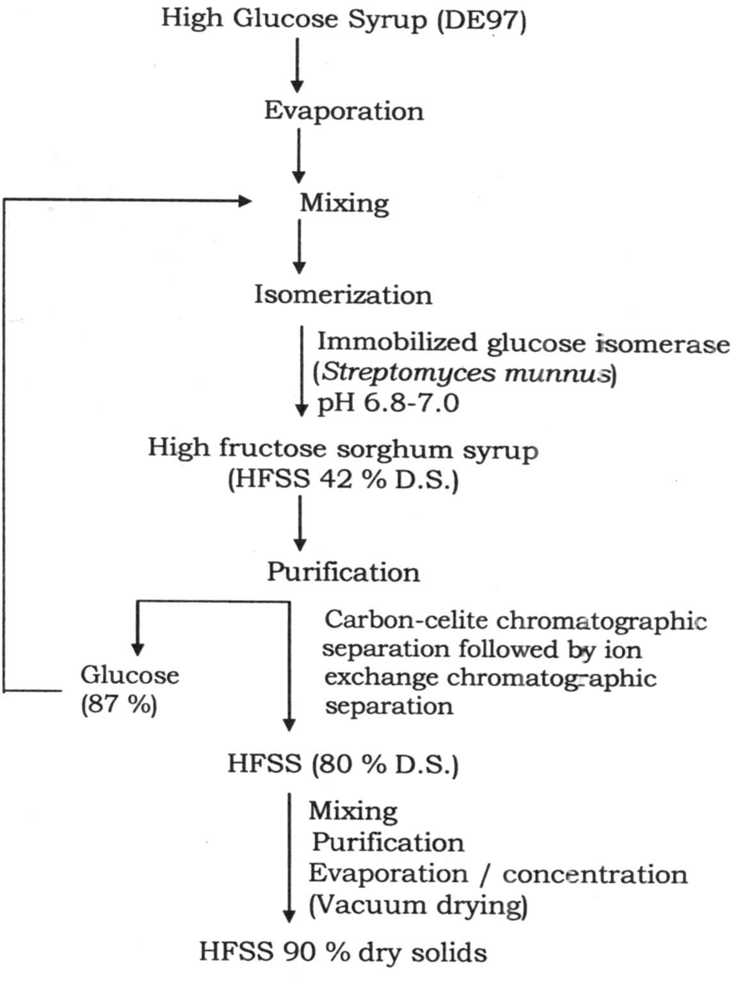

Figure 15b. Production of high fructose syrup using immobilized glucoisomerase (*Streptomyces munnus*) at optimum experimental conditions

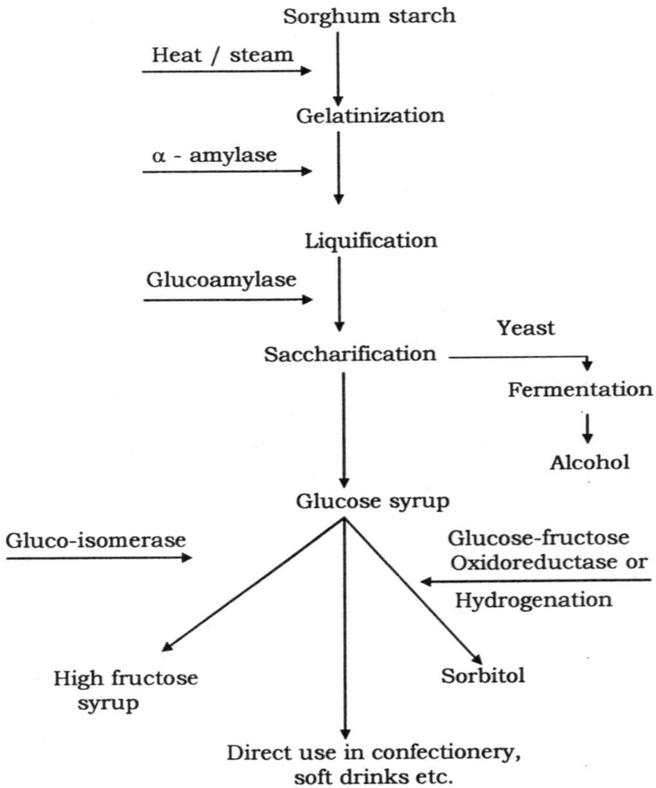

Figure 15c. Sweetener production from starch

Table 63. Physico-chemical properties of high fructose syrup.

Parameter	HFSS from CSH-18	HFS control (glucose)
Refractive index	1.453	1.455
Colour	Yellowish	Whitish yellow
Dry solids (%)	67.93	70.00
Moisture (%)	32.06	30.00
Ash (%)	0.08	0.05
Acidity (%)	0.11	0.09
^{0}Brix (TSS, %)	58.33	60.00

5. Production of sorbitol from sorghum starch

Sorbitol solution appears to be a clear, colourless and syrupy liquid with pleasantly sweet taste. The solution was essentially odourless. The sorbitol content of the solution was found to be 66 per cent (Table 64). Study of the composition of the prepared solution revealed that the solution contents 0.21 per cent reducing sugars and 0.70 per cent total sugars. In order to assess the importance and feasibility in food and other industries, the viscosity profile of sorbitol solution is considered as one of the important parameters. Sorbitol being a monosaccharide polyol, contributes little to the viscosity of the solution to which it is added. The viscosity of sorbitol solution over a wide range of shear rates and temperature has been carried out by using Haake's Rotoviscometer (RV 20). The flow behaviour of sorbitol solution at various temperatures (20 - 26 ^{0}C) was investigated. The results indicated that the viscosity of the sorbitol solution linearly decreases with the increase in the temperature and shear rate (Table 65).

Various functional properties of sorbitol were extensively studied. The refractive index of the solution (at 20 ^{0}C) was found to be 1.45. The relative sweetness of the 10 per cent solution was compared with the sweetness of standard sucrose. The relative sweetness of the solution was found to be 60:100. The data on the cooling effect of the solution revealed that the solution gives cooling effect within six seconds of putting it in mouth. The solution was found to be thermally stable up to 160 - 180 ^{0}C (Table 66). The flash point of the sorbitol solution was found to be 300 ^{0}C and the specific gravity of the solution was 1.28 at 25 ^{0}C. The non-carcinogenic properties of sorbitol are making it increasing accepted sweetener in the insulin-independent mechanism of sorbitol make it an ideal sweetener for the diabetes. Sorbitol produced from sorghum starch hydrolyzes by chemical hydrogenation in presence of nickel catalyst and was used as sweetener. The milk chocolate prepared by using sucrose had scored higher value for all the quality attributes than the milk chocolates prepared by using sorbitol and sucrose in combination. Milk chocolate manufactured from sorbitol resulted in low-viscosity chocolate base, which was corrected by using additives (starch or guar gum 2 per cent).

Table 64. Biochemical properties of sorbitol solution

Parameter	Observations
Appearance	Clear, colourless, syrup liquid
Colour	Watery white
Taste	Pleasantly sweet
Odour	Essentially odourless
Assay (%) D-sorbitol	66.0
Reducing sugars (%)	0.21
Total sugars (%)	0.70
Residues on ignition (%)	0.10
Water (%)	29.5
pH (10 % solution)	6.5

Table 65. Viscosity profile for sorbitol syrup.

Temperature (^{0}C)	Apparent viscosity (Cps) Shear rate (S^1)			
	4.51	**34.73**	**97.41**	**451**
20	160	147	132	98
30	110	105	88	71
40	80	72	66	49
50	65	58	48	34
60	55	47	32	20

Table 66. Functional properties of sorbitol solution.

Parameter	Observations
Refractive index (20 ^{0}C)	1.45
Relative sweetness (10 % solution)	60:100
Cooling effect	In 6 seconds
Thermal stability	160-180 ^{0}C
Flash point	Above 300 ^{0}C
Specific gravity at 25 ^{0}C	1.28

6. Bio-ethanol production

At present, there are three important routes for producing bioethanol:

1. From starch or sugar crops,
2. From cellulose following enzymatic hydrolysis and
3. From cellulose following chemical hydrolysis.

The cost of production of bioethanol from the three routes is comparable. However, commercial production is based on starch and sugar crops only; there is no full-scale production plant based on cellulose.

Billions of liters of bioethanol is produced annually mostly in Brazil (from sugarcane) and USA (from maize). The process based on sugarcane has low productivity and the enormous amount of cellulosic bagasse is either burnt or ploughed back into soil; this biomass is a potential source of bioethanol.

Sugarcane, Sugar beet, Sweet sorghum etc. provide a good substrate. Juices from these crops contain sugar, e.g., sugarcane juice has about 12% fermentable sugars, and can be used directly for fermentation. Molasses, sweet sorghum syrup and spent sulphite liquor are the most common substrates. Molasses (C grade) obtained after sugar recovery contains about 35% sucrose, 19% other reducing agents and 14% other organic substances; thus the total fermentable sugars are nearly 50-55%. Molasses is first suitably diluted, then treated with 0.5% by weight concentrated sulphuric acid at 70-95 ^{0}c (mainly for removal of calcium salts and acidification) and used for fermentation. Cereals like maize, wheat, sorghum etc. contain 60-75% w/w starch, which on hydrolysis produces glucose in the ratio 9:10 (Figure 16, Plate 13).

Starch
(e.g. powdered seed meal, tubers etc.)

↓ ← Enzyme hydrolysis
(50-60 ^{0}C)

Glucose

↓ ← Yeast
Glycolysis (30-35 ^{0}C)

Pyruvate

↓ ← Yeast (30-35 ^{0}C)
(Pyruvate decarboxylase)

Acetaldehyde

↓ ← Yeast (30-35 ^{0}C)
Alcohol dehydrogenase

Ethanol
(Recovered by distillation)

Figure 16. Flow chart for the production of ethanol from a starch substrate.

Generally, starch is a mixture of amylose (20-30%; water soluble linear polymer) and amylopectin (70-80%; water insoluble branched polymer). A cooking process aided by enzymes usually achieves conversion of starch into glucose. Seeds are powdered and the resulting meal is mixed with water in the ratio of 1:2.5 - 3. α-amylase is then added and the temperature is raised by steam injection to 105-110 ^{0}c and held for about 20 min. During this period, starch grains become dissolved to form a viscous suspension (gelatinization) due to the cooking effect of heat. At the same time α-amylase digests partially some of the starch molecules; this reduces the viscosity of the suspension; this is called liquefaction. The suspension contains solubilized starch molecules, and dextrins (short chains of glucose units). The suspension called mash is cooled to 85-90 ^{0}c and more α-amylase is added to complete the process of liquification (for 90 min). The total dose of α-amylase is about 1.5kg/ton starch. The mash is cooled to 55-60 ^{0}c and 1.5-3.5 liter glucoamylase/ton of starch is added to produce glucose from dextrins and maltose. The reaction duration is usually 2 days, and it achieves the dextrose equivalent of 99. Saccharification by glucoamylase continues during the fermentation.

Proper fermentation of 100g glucose by selected strains of *Saccharomyces cerevisiae* and *Saccharomyces carlsbergensis* yields 45-49g bioethanol, the theoretical limit being 51.1g. ($C_6H_{12}O_6 \longrightarrow 2C_2H_5OH + 2CO_2$). For the fermentation process batch or continuous processes are used. Batch process is the most commonly used. Ammonium sulphate or Urea (N source) and a salt of phosphoric acid (P source) are added to the substrate. Most commonly the temperature during fermentation is 32-38 ^{0}C and pH is between 4.5-5.0.

As the ethanol level rises, both ethanol production and yeast cell growth are progressively inhibited, and eventually cells begin to die.

In general, yeast growth stops at 6-9% w/v ethanol, but ethanol production, at least in some strains, may continue upto 15% ethanol or higher. Ethanol inhibition can be relieved by continuous removal of ethanol. Ethanol recovery is based on distillation.

a. The broth is distilled in a beer column to yield 85% v/v ethanol.

b. The next step of rectification gives 96.5% ethanol, which is then.

c. Dehydrated to 99.4% using benzene or cyclohexane if the ethanol is to be used as a fuel blend.

The wastewater effluent can be used directly on land, used for anaerobic digestion for methane generation, evaporated to dry syrup for animal feed or fuel or used as substrate for fungal biomass production.

Chapter **25**

Nutritional and Keeping Quality

The objective of making all food items mentioned in this book is to increase the consumption of sorghum and millets. All the above products mentioned are having better nutritional quality in terms of protein, fiber, minerals and vitamins as they are made from sorghum and other millets. These products also have a slow digestibility and the products other than sweets are ideal for diabetic and obese populations of the society.

The keeping quality of the various products varies depending on the ingredients present and method of preparation. The keeping quality of break fast foods is minimum one day, however, the batter of idli and dosa can be stored for two days in refrigerator. The keeping quality of Lunch items is minimum one day. Jowar roti can be stored for two to three days and up to six days in refrigerator. Annam, Sankạti, and Ambali can be stored only for one day. The keeping quality of sorghum sweets is minimum two days, but the kesari, kheer, burffi, sweet rolls in milk can be stored for only one day and if stored in refrigerator it will be two days. Rawa laddu can be stored for fifteen days. The keeping quality of sorghum snack foods is minimum ten days, but the pakoda, can be stored for three days only. Garelu (vada), and punugulu, kudumulu can be stored for two days. The remaining items chekkalu, murukulu, fryums, and namakpara can be stored for fifteen to twenty days.

Chapter 26

Health Foods of Sorghum and Present Market Status

Sorghum with its nutritionally rich parameters (dietary fibre, slow digestibility of starch & protein, minerals and lack of gluten) makes essential health foods. Colored sorghums with the presence of polyphenols, which are known to be antioxidants, are also regarded as health foods. Antioxidants are known for improving immunity and also preventing cardiovascular diseases and cancer. Colored sorghums are gaining importance as a source of antioxidants in U.S.A.

Processed foods and instant food mixes based on jowar are receiving attention in different parts of country in India. For example instant dosa mix made from jowar is being marketed in Coimbatore in Tamilnadu. Contact details are given below. In Zaheerabad, Andhra Pradesh in Deccan Society (a NGO) is popularizing millet foods through a shop namely 'Café Ethnic'. Sorghum and all kinds of millets are used to make different traditional foods and are made available here.

The biscuits based on jowar along with other cereals and soybean marketed with the label 'Nurtrient –Diet' by Alsa agro tech private Limited, Moosarambagh, Hyderabad.

The various health foods are listed below:

1. Manna Health Mix; Marketed by Saga Food Products Pvt, ltd; Tamil Nadu;
2. Pusti, the health mix : Manufactured and marketed by Pusti, CBM compound Vishakhapatnam.
3. Nutriment- Diet: biscuits manufactured by Alsa agro tech private limited, Moosarambagh, Hyderabad.
4. Instant jowar *dosa* mix: Karthik Cottage, Kaveri salai, Selvapuram, Coimbatore-641 026.
5. Sunira foods Private limited.

Chapter 27

Conclusions

Sorghum grain with its rich nutritional qualities like high dietary fibre, minerals and slow digestibility of starch and protein is having great potential for incorporation in all possible Indian foods, both traditional and novel foods. Sorghum grain is also having potential to make *rawa* /semolina, flakes and noodles apart from pops. Sorghum rawa and flour are made into different food products that are having great importance in Indian breakfast, lunch and snack food, replacing the usual fine cereal rice and wheat. Like maize, sorghum flour can be processed into different kinds of extruded products through extruder machines. For the nutritional enrichment cereal flours including sorghum are blended with soybean and protein could be enriched up to 14% in the composite flour. The composite flour is ideal to make all bakery foods like cakes and biscuits. Instant food mixes are also possible to prepare from sorghum rawa and flour. Health drinks based on sorghum malt along with other millet malts with added flavours and preservatives are prepared. Recently, health foods based on sorghum are available in market in the form of biscuits and health mixes.

Chapter **28**

Future Research Work Needed on Sorghum

---

1. Dehulling of moulded grains and marketing
2. Mix flours preparations for improvement in the nutritional quality
3. Popularization as a health and nutraceutical food
4. Food industries should come forward to use sorghum in various food products
5. In plant training/demonstrations to women/youths
6. More publication for popularization through different media (Radio, TV, Magazines, Scientific Journals, Books etc)
7. To accelerate research and extension for use of refined sorghum flour for high fiber bread and biscuits
8. Develop literature on health benefits of sorghum for wide circulation
9. Setting up of demonstration plant for production of different sorghum food products such as bread, biscuits, malted flours, starch, beer, ethanol etc. from sorghum
10. Seminars with group of medical doctors, lions clubs, rotary clubs, NGOs to emphasize the health benefits of sorghum in elderly diets
11. Every person should consume sorghum at least 3 times in week and acts a link between farmers and health food store/doctors.
12. To popularize health benefits of sorghum and make available processed sorghum flour to masses
13. Promote farmers to produce organic sorghum and popularize it for health benefits among urbanites so that farmers get better income and motivation for sorghum farming

Action plan needed for promotion of sorghum products in India

Short term (1-3 years)	Long term (3-5 years)
Awareness creation and generic promotion of sorghum products	Generic promotion of sorghum-products through print and electronic media
Training of rural/urban individuals and/or groups at domestic level sorghum processing for food uses	Development of sorghum varieties with specific end uses (Food/Products/Pharmaceutical)
Human resource and entrepreneurship developments in sorghum food products	Application of recent food processing technology such as extrusion cooking, high pressure membrane separation, enzyme processing, SCF extraction, microwave heating etc. to have newer and diversified sorghum-products for food and feed also
Preparation and notification of quality standards for sorghum-food products	Development of sorghum-based specialty food products
Establishment of sorghum food enterprises for manufacturing and marketing of sorghum foods	Formation of sorghum-foods manufactures Association of India to take care of large scale sorghum-food manufacturing and marketing in India and abroad
Sorghum-foods enhance human health at an affordable cost. Hence the need is to promote sorghum-based foods for all and by all means.	

Chapter **29**

References

Au, P. M. and Fields, M. L. 1981. Nutritive quality of fermented sorghum. J. Food Sci. 46: 652-654.

Badi, S. M. and Hoseney, R. C. 1976. Use of sorghum and pearl millet flours in cookies. Ceréal Chem. 53: 733-738.

Bankar, J. R., Chavan, J. K. and Kadam, S. S. 1986. Effect of grain conditioning on physico-chemical properties of sorghum bhakari. J. Maharashtra Agric. Univ., 11: 221-223.

Bender, A. E. 1973. Composition of infant foods, In Nutritional and Dietetic Foods, International Textbook Co. Ltd., London, U. K., p. 64.

Chavan, J. K. and Kadam S. S. 1989. Nutritional improvement of cereals by fermentation. CRC in Food Sci. and Nut. 28: 349-399.

Chavan, J. K. and Salunkhe, D. K. 1984. Structure of sorghum grain. In Nutritional and processing quality of sorghum. Pp. 21-31.

Chavan, J. K., Chavan, U. D. and Nagarkar, V. D. 1989. Effect of malting and fermentation on nutritional quality of sorghum. J. Maharashtra Agric. Univ., 14: 246-247.

Chavan, U.D. (1987). "Effect of Fermentation on the Nutritional Quality of Grain Sorghum (*Sorghum bicolour* L. Moench). "M. Sc. (Agric.) Thesis, Mahatma Phule Agriculture University Rahuri, Maharashtra, INDIA. pp.i-95.

Chavan, U.D. and Chavan, J.K. (1992). Utilization of groundnut flour in preparation of sorghum bhakari. J. Maharashtra Agric. Univ., 17 (20) : 346-347.

Chavan, U.D., Chavan, J.K. and Kadam, S.S. (1988). Effect of fermentation on soluble proteins and *in-vitro* protein digestibility of sorghum, green gram and sorghum + green gram blends. J. Food Sci. 53 : 1574-1575.

Chavan, U. D. and Chavan, J. K. 1991. Utilization of malted sorghum, mung bean and black gram in preparation of bhakari. J. Maharashtra Agric. Univ., 16: 141-142.

Chevassua-Agnes, S., Favier, J. C. and Joseph, A. 1976. Traditional technology and nutritive value of sorghum beer from camaoon (in French) Cah. Nutr. Diet. 11: 89-104.

Desikachar, H. S. R. 1977. Processing of sorghum and millets for versatile food uses in India. In Sorghum and millets for human food. Pp. 41-45. Symp. Proc. IACC, Vienna, 1976. Tropical Products Institute, London.

Hahn, R. R. 1969. Dry milling of grain sorghum. Cereal Sci. Today. 14: 234-237.

Karim, A. and Rooney, L. W. 1972. Characterization of pentosans in sorghum grain. J. Food Sci. 37: 369-371.

Kazanas, N. and Fields, M. L. 1981. Nutritional improvement of sorghum by fermentation. J. Food Sci. 46: 819-821.

Miller, O. H. and Burns, E. E. 1970. Starch characteristics of selected grain sorghum as related to human food. J. Food Sci. 35: 666-668.

Murty, D. S., Patil, H. D., Prasad Rao, K. E. and House, L. R. 1982. A note on screening the Indian sorghum collection for popping quality. J. Food Sci. Technol. 19: 79-80.

Murty, D. S. and Subramanian, V. 1982. Sorghum roti. I. Traditional methods of consumption and standard procedures for evaluation. ICRISAT, 1982, Proc, Intl. Symp. On Sorghum grain quality. 28-31 October, 1981, Patancheru, A.P. India. Pp. 73-78.

Novellie, L. 1977. Beverages from sorghum and millets in "Proc. of Symp. On Sorghum and Millets for Human Food". International Association for Cereal Chemistry. Symposium. Vienna. 1976. Tropical Products Institute, London. Pp. 73-77.

Odunfa, S. A., Nordsrom, J. and Adeniran, S. A. 1994. Development of starter cultures for nutrient enrichment of ogia West African fermented cereal gruel. Report submitted to HBVC research grants program. USAID, Washington, U.S.A.

Patil, U. S, Dalvi, U. S. and Chavan, J. K. 2003. Studies on the production of starch from mould infected discolored sorghum. J. Food Sci. Technol. 40: 115-117.

Raghavandra Rao, S. N. and Desikachar, H. S. R. 1964. Pearling as a method of refining jower and wheat and its effect on their chemical composition. J. Food Sci. Technol. 1: 40-42.

Raghavandra Rao, S. N., Malleshi, N. G., Sreedharamurty, S., Viraktamath, C. S. and Desikachar, H. S. R. 1979. Characteristics of roti, dosa and vermicelli from maize, sorghum and bajra. J. Food Sci. Technol. 16: 21-24.

Reichert, R. D. and Young, C. G. 1976. Dehulling cereal grains and grain legumes for developing countries. I. Quantities comparison between attrition and abrasive type mills. Cereal Chem. 53: 829-839.

Salunkhe, D. K., Kadam, S. S. and Chavan, J. K. 1977. Nutritional quality of proteins in grain sorghum. Qual. Plant. Pl. Foods Human Nutr. 27: 187-205.

Schrimshaw, N. S. 1974. Nutritional requirements for high protein foods, Proc. Int. Symp. Protein Foods and Concentrates, Central Food Technol. Res. Institute, Mysore, India, pp. 13-18.

Shepherd, A. D. 1974. How grain structure influences sorghum quality, presented to 5th E. African Cereals Res. Conf. Malawi.

Sullins, R. D. and Rooney, L. W. 1974. Microscopic evaluation of the digestibility of sorghum lines that differ in endosperm characteristics. Cereal Chem. 51: 134–142.

Sulllins, R. D., Rooney, L. W. and Rosenow, D. T. 1975. The endosperm structure of high lysine sorghum. Crop Sci. 15: 599-600.

Wang, Y. D. and Fields, M. L. 1987. Germination of corn and sorghum in the home to improve nutritive value. J. Food Sci. 43: 1113-1115.

Watson, S. A. 1970. Wet milling process and products. In Sorghum production and utilization. J. S. Wall and Ross, W. M. Eds. The AVI Publishing Co. Inc, Westport, Connecticut USA. Pp. 602-626.

APPENDEX - I

Conversion factors (weights and measures)

Length	1 m	10^{10} A	39.37 in	3.2808 ft
Area	1 m^2	10^4 cm^2	1550.0031 in^2	10.7639 ft^2
Volume	1 m^3	1000 L	10^6 cm^3	264.17 gal (US)
Mass	1 kg	2.2046 lbm	35.274 oz	1.1023 x 10^{-3} ton (short)
Density	1 g/cm^3	1000 kg/m^3	62.428 lbm/ft^3	8.3454 lbm/ gal (US)
Velocity	1 m/s	3.6 km/h	2.2369 min/h	196.85 ft/min
Force	1 kg-m/s^2 (N)	0.2248 lbf	10^5 g.cm/s^2 (dyn)	7.2330 lbm.ft/ s^2 (pdf)
Pressure	1 atm	101.325 kg/ms^2 (pa)	14.696 lbf/in^2 (psi)	760 mm Hg
Energy	1 kg.m^2/s^2 (J)	9.4782 x 10^{-4} Btu	0.2388 cal	0.7376 ft.lbf
Power	1 J/S (W)	1 kg/m^2/s^3	3.4121 Btu/h	1.341 x 10^{-3} hp
Thermal conductivity	1 W/m.k	0.5778 Btu/h.A.^{0}F	2.388 x 10^{-3} cal/s.cm.^{0}C	6.9335 Btu.in/h.ft^2.^{0}F
Specific heat	1 KJ/kg.K	0.2388 cal/g.^{0}C	0.2388 Btf/lbm.^{0}F	185.86 ft.lbf/lbm.^{0}F
Viscosity (dynamic)	1 pa.S	1 kg/m.s	1000 cp	0.6720 lbm/ft.S
Temperature	^{0}C=5/9 (F-32)	^{0}F = 9/5 (^{0}C) + 32	K = ^{0}C + 273.15	^{0}R = ^{0}F + 45967

APPENDEX - II

Agricultural Related Websites

http://www.nrcsorghum.res.in
http://www.aau.ac.in
http://www.mpkv.nic.in
http://www.hau.nic.in
http://www.csauk.org
http://www.pdkv.mah.nic.in
http://www.gud.guj.nic.in
http://www.mpkv.mah.nic.in
http://www.hpkv.nic.in
http://www.icar.org.in/sherk/welcome.htm
http://www.gny.ifas.uf.edu
http://www.agri.surf.com
http://www.agfind.com
http://www.morrisville.edu/njc
http://www.agr.ca/agnweb/agmweb.htm
http://www.agri.infolink.com
http://virtualquincy.com/quincy/ag/agricultural.
http://www.icar.org.in
http://www.iaripusa.org
http://www.cishlko.org.
http://www.cri.ogr
http://www.cpri.hp.nic.in
http://www.cpri.nic.in
http://www.kar.nic.in
http://www.kar.nic.in/cashew
http://www.nic.map.org
http://www.hocmushroom.org
http://www.cazri.nic.in
http://www.ndri.nic.in

http://www.nbsslup.org
http://www.nbpgr.delhi.nic.in
http://www.nic.ipm.org
http://www.dor_icar.org
http://www.icar_org.in/dwr/dwrmain
http://www.cswri.raj.nic.in
http://www.cirg.nic.in
http://www.cicr.india.org
http://www.rice.india.tripool.com
http://www.upgov.up.nic.in
http://www.amazon.com
http://www.servtech.c. (Digital Library)
http://www.leweb.gov/. (The Library of Congress)
http://www.Thorplus.Lib.purdue.edu/vlibrzy (The virtual Library)
http://www.nal.usda.gov./NAL (National Agricultural Library)
http://www.Fao.hg/Library/Librs.htm. (FAO-Library)
http://www.Cobweb Common Wealth Agricultural Bureau
http://www.ioe.org - Journal of Extension
http://www.progressive farmers.com – Progressive farmers
http://www.agecon.ugd.edu/jab-Journal of Agribusiness
http://www.agecom.uga.edu/jade/-Journal of Agriculture and applied economic
http://www.agrivareers.com
http://www.agrilaunch.com
http://www.agriculture online.com
http://www.cgiar.org
http://www.kisan.net
http://www.myrada.org
http://www.nads.edu
http://www.fao.org

http://www.wellcent
http://www.apeda.com
http://www.falbazar.com
http://www.herbal.com
http://www.ecobot.coms
http://www.agri.gov.ab'ca/crops/badimarketing.com
http://www.hortibizindia.nic.in
http://www.mofpi.nic.in
http://www.farmersshaw.net/chei/coneers
http://www.agnet.co.uk.agsan.htm
http://www.infolink.com
http://www.aginfonet/sk.ca
http://www.msamb.com
http://www.aqriwatch.com
http://www.agmarket.nic.in

APPENDIX - III

About Sorghum Improvement Project, Mahatma Phule Krishi Vidyapeeth, Rahuri.

The Sorghum Improvement Project is started at Mahatma Phule Krishi Vidyapeet, Rahuri in 1973 with following major objectives.

1. To develop new genotypes and hybrids in *rabi* sorghum.
2. To develop advanced agricultural technology for cultivation of *rabi* sorghum for higher yield and quality.
3. To develop sorghum genotypes for alternative uses such as sweet sorghum for ethanol production and other alternative uses.

Scientists working at Sorghum Improvement Project have developed various new *rabi* and alternative uses sorghum genotypes as given below:

New Genotype	Year of release	Grain yield (q/ha)	Fodder yield (q/ha)	Remarks/ Recommended
A. New genotypes for grain and fodder purpose				
Swati	1984	24-28	50-60	Dryland/Irrigated
Selection - 3	1994	5-6	15-18	Shallow soil
Phule Yashoda	1998	20-25	70-75	Irrigated area
Phule Maulee	1999	8-9 15-20	20-25 50-60	Shallow soil Medium soil
Phule Chitra	2006	20-25	55-60	Medium soil
Vasudha	2007	30-35	70-75	Deep & irrigated soil
CSV - 22	2007	24-28	65-70	Deep soil, irrigated
Anuradha	2008	8-10	30-35	Shallow, dryland condition
RSV 1006	2008	40-50	90-100	Irrigated, Deep soil
B. New genotypes for alternative uses				
SSV 84	1991	10-12	300-350 (green)	Sweet sorghum for ethanol
CSV 19 SS	2004	10-15	350-400 (green)	Sweet sorghum for ethanol
Phule Amruta	2003	-	450-500 (green)	Green fodder, Irrigated condition
Phule Uttara	2005	20-25	50-60	For Hurda
RPOSV 3	-	12-15	30-35	For pops
RPASV 3	-	8-10	30-35	For papad

APPEDEX-IV

Equipments required for processing of Grain Sorghum

Sr. No.	Name of the equipment	No. of items	Purpose	Approximate cost (Rs.)
A. Preparation of bakery products				
1.	Dehuller/Decorticator	1	Dehulling all types of grains and millets	80,000=00
2.	Grain grinding mill	1	For grinding grains to get flour for preparation of various types of products	15,000=00
3.	Sieve set	1 set	For getting various types of flours for different products	60,000=00
4.	Dough mixer (cap. 5 kg)	1	For mixing various types of fours and preparation of dough	80,000=00
5.	Dough divider	1	For getting required amount of dough for breads, buns etc.	50,000=00
6.	Molding machine	1	For molding dough for bread making	40,000=00
7.	Bread molds/boxes	100	For baking breads in oven	25,000=00
8.	Baking oven (single deck)	1	For baking various types of bakery products	80,000=00
9.	Bread slicer	1	For making slices of bread	40,000=00
10.	Sealing machine	1	For sealing breads packets	20,000=00
11.	Sugar grinding mill	1	For sugar grinding	25,000=00
12.	Biscuits molding machine	1	For preparation of biscuits and cookies	1,00,000=00

13.	Different size biscuits and cookies dies	50	For to prepare various types of biscuits and cookies	45,000=00
14.	Biscuits and cookies trays	100	For baking biscuits and cookies	10,000=00
B. Preparation of extruded products				
15.	Extruder-single arm with different dies and cutters	1	For preparation of noodles	2,25,000=00
16.	Extruder-twin arm with different dies and cutters	1	For macaroni and spaghetti, vermicelli and 3-D snacks	4,50,000=00
17.	Tray dryer	1	For drying various types of products	75,000=00
18.	Papad making machine	1	For preparation of papads	50,000=00
C. Preparation of weaning and baby food products				
19.	*Roti/Bhakari* making machine	1	For preparation of *Roti/Bhakari*	80,000=00
20.	Germinator	1	For malting grains	75,000=00
21.	Fermenter	1	For fermentation of various grains flours	1,00,000=00
D. Common items required for above product preparations				
22.	Weighing balance a. 400 g capacity and b. 5 kg capacity	 1 1	For getting required quantity of raw material for preparation of various types processed products	75,000=00
23.	Water purifier/Water softener	1	For getting filtered water	40,000=00
24.	Refrigerators	2	For to keep chemicals/yeast etc.	25,000=00
25.	Vacuum packing machine	1	For sealing various types of dry products	60,000=00

26.	Nitrogen flushing and Sealing machine	1	For to extend the shelf life of product	1,50,000=00
27.	Microwave oven	1	For baking various food products	15,000=00
28.	Food Processor	1	For processing various food products	10,000=00
29.	Stainless steel top working tables (3 Nos.), (8′ x 4′ x 3′, L. W. H)	3	For working and processing various products	90,000=00
30.	Mini Dhal mill	1	For preparation of dhal from various types of pulses	1,00,000=00
31.	Naylon dhori dhal polisher	1	For polishing dhal	70,000=00
32.	Besan flour mill	1	For preparation of besan flour from pulse dhal	50,000=00
33.	Semolina/Rava mill	1	For preparation of semolina/ Rava from cereal grains	25,000=00
34.	Pop corn machine	1	For preparation of pop from various cereal grains	50,000=00
35.	Rice mill	1	For rice milling to get good quality rice	1,00,000=00
36.	Materials and supplies	-	For raw material, chemicals, yeast, utensils, mislaginous items etc.	1,00,000=00
			Total	**26,85,000=00**

APPENDEX – V

Websites for Nutritional Information

http://www.users.rcn.com/jkimball.ma.ultrnet/BiologyPages/N/Nutrition.html

http://www. Ars.usda.gov/ba/bhnrc.

http://www.asinut.net

http://www.globnut.net

http://www.nutrition.otago.ac.nc

http://www.mrc-hnr.cam.aguk/

http://www.cumc.cdumbia.edu/deptlihn

http://www.faoorg/docrep/W8079E/W8079E00.htm

http://www.fshn.uiuc.edu

http://www.blackwellpublishing.com/journals/jhn

http://www.COREgroup.org

http://www.DevelopmentGateway.org

http://www.suhrs.dk

http://www.MonsterIndia.com

http://www.hnrc.tufts.edu

http://www.ars.usda.gov/research/programs/programs.htm?NP_CODE=107

http://www.grad.ubc.ca/apply/programs

http://www.gla.ac.uk/departments/humannutrition/index.html

http://www.uchsc.edu/nutrition

http://www3.open.ac.uk/courses/bin/p12.

http://www.stfx.ca/academic/human-nutrition

http://www.itana2002.org

APPENDEX – VI

PROJECT REPORT (STANDARD FORMAT)

OF

PROCESSING INDUSTRIES

1. Primary information

a. Name of Unit : ....

b. Units' address ....

c. Constitution :..

d. Name of proprietor :..

e. Birth date, Age :..

f. Qualification :..

g. Nature of business :..

h. Registration No. of business :..

i. Loan for :..

j. Loan amount :..

2. Introduction

In this section the information on following pcints should be included:

a. Experience of the proprietor in this field

b. Facilities and arrangement for product sale

c. Information regarding machinery requirement and their availability as well as importance

d. Availability of the skilled and unskilled labour

e. Information regarding self-sale counter

f. Importance of this business to the society

3. Scope of business

Give the location of the processing unit and availability of raw material in that area. Provide the information regarding marketing of the processed product.

4. Manufacturing process

Give the details of manufacturing process/technology employed.

5. Land

Land for proprietor owns unit or it is in partnership give details. If in partnership then make agreement and submit with this proposal.

6. Building

Give the details about building construction (shed, RCC or load bearing etc.).

7. Water supply

Water supply from bore well or Municipal Corporation etc.

8. Electric power supply

MSEB connection deposit, main switchboard, wiring, fitting, tubes, fans, labour charges etc.

9. Printing

For labeling, advertisement, specification on the product etc.

10. Furniture

Expenditure occurred on tables, chairs, cupboards, stools etc.

11. QUANTITATIVE DETAILS

(Rs. In Lacs)

Sr. No.	Description	1st year	2nd year	3rd year	4th year	5th year
1.	Installed capacity 300 days & 20 hrs					
2.	Utilization of capacity (%)					
3.	Raw material consumption at installed capacity (Rs./Ton)					

4.	Sale at installed capacity (Rate Rs. / Ton)					
5.	Raw material consumption at utilized capacity					
6.	Sales at utilized capacity					

12. CALCULATION OF WORKING CAPITAL

Sr. No.	Particular	Holding period (days)	Amount
1.	Raw material		
2.	Consumable packing		
3.	Finished goods		
4.	Other Exp.		
5.	Debtors		
Gross current assets:			
6.	Less credits		
	Net working capital		
	Own margin	35 or 25%	
	Bank Finance	56 or 75%	

13. COST OF PROJECT AND SOURCES OF FINANCE

Sr. No.	Item	Cost already incurred	Cost to be incurred	Total
A. Cost of project:				
1.	Land			
2.	Site development			
3.	Civil & Technical work			
4.	Plant & Machinery			
5.	Total working capital			
6.	Preliminary & preoperative Exp. (Bank fee, mortgage fee, Prof. Fee etc.)			
	Total			

B. Source of finance:				
1.	Equity capital			
2.	Subsidy/Quasi equity			
3.	Others			
4.	Unsecured Loan			
5.	Term Loan			
	Total			

14. PROJECT PROFIT AND LOSS ACCOUNT

(Rs. In Lacs)

Sr. No.	Particular	1St year	2nd year	3rd year	4th year	5th year
1.	Gross sales					
2.	Job work charges					
A.	Net sales					
B. Cost of production						
1.	Raw material (as per qty. details)					
2.	Power & Fuel					
3.	Direct labour & Wages					
4.	Consumables stores					
5.	Repair & Maintenance					
6.	Other Mfg. Exp.					
7.	Depreciation					
8.	Add opening stock in process & finished goods					
9.	Deduct closing stock in process & finished goods					
C	Cost of sales					
D	Gross profit (A- C)					
E	Interest					
F	General & administrative over					
G	Profit before Tax					

H	Provision for Tax					
I	Net Profit					
J	Depression added back					
K	Net cash accruals					
L	Repayment obligations					
M	Debt service ratio (Average DSCR 3.87)					

15. PROJECTED BALANCE SHEET

Sr. No.	Particular	1St year	2nd year	3rd year	4th year	5th year
A. Assets						
1.	Fixed assets					
2.	Investment/L. C. Deposits					
3.	Current assets					
	a. Raw material, packing Exp.					
	b. Finished goods					
	c. Debtors					
	d. Other current assets					
	Total					
B. Liabilities						
1.	Equity capital					
2.	Profit & loss A/C					
3.	Unsecured Loans					
4.	Quasi equity					
5.	Subsidy (Fr. MFPI)					
6.	Secured Loans					
7.	Working limits Fr. Bank					
1.	Term Loan					
2.	Creditors					
3.	Other current Liab. & Provision					
	Total					

16. PROJECTED CASH FLOW AND FUND FLOW STATEMENT

Sr. No.	Particular	1St year	2nd year	3rd year	4th year	5th year
A. Sources						
1.	Net cash accruals					
2.	Subsidy					
	Total					
B. Application						
1.	Repayment of term Loan					
2.	Repayment of unsecured & quasi equity					
3.	Increase in investment					
4.	Increase in W. C.					
	Total					

17. PROJECTED BREAKEVEN

(Rs. In Lacs)

1.	Fixed cost (Average)		
2.	Average selling price		
3.	Average variable cot (per ton)		
	a. Materials		
	b. Labours		
	c. Other overheads		
4.	Contribution/Unit		
5.	Breakeven qty		
6.	Breakeven value		
7.	Percentage on installed capacity		

18. REPAYMENT SCHEDULE OF TERM LOAN & INTEREST ON TERM LOAN

Period	Principle amount	Interest	Total
Interest in ....%, period in quarters			
1st Year			
I Quarter			
II Quarter			
III Quarter			
IV Quarter			
Total			
2nd Year			
I Quarter			
II Quarter			
III Quarter			
IV Quarter			
Total			
3rd Year			
I Quarter			
II Quarter			
III Quarter			
IV Quarter			
Total			
4th Year			
I Quarter			
II Quarter			
III Quarter			
IV Quarter			
Total			
5th Year			
I Quarter			
II Quarter			
III Quarter			
IV Quarter			
Total			
Grand Total			

19. CALCULATION OF DEPRECIATION AS PER I. T. RULES & W.D.V. METHOD

Period	Building	Plant and Machinery	Total
Initial			
1st Year			
Total			
2nd Year			
Total			
3rd Year			
Total			
4th Year			
Total			
5th Year			
Total			

20. LIST OF PLANT AND MACHINERY

Sr. No.	Name of Plant or Machinery	Price (Rs.)	Quantity (Nos.)	Total amount (Rs.)
1.				
2.				
3.				
4.				
5.				
6.				
7.				
8.				
9.				
10.				
	Total			

21. TOTAL INTEREST PAYABLE YEARWISE

Period	Term	Working	Other	Total
@ p. a.	11%	15%	18%	
1st year				
2nd year				
3rd Year				
4th Year				
5th Year				
Total				

22. SALARY AND WAGES DETAILS

Sr. No.	Particular	Nos.	Salary p.m.	Total
1.	Operator			
2.	Skilled workers			
3.	Unskilled workers			
	Total			

Proprietor/Partner
(Name & Address of the Unit)

Index

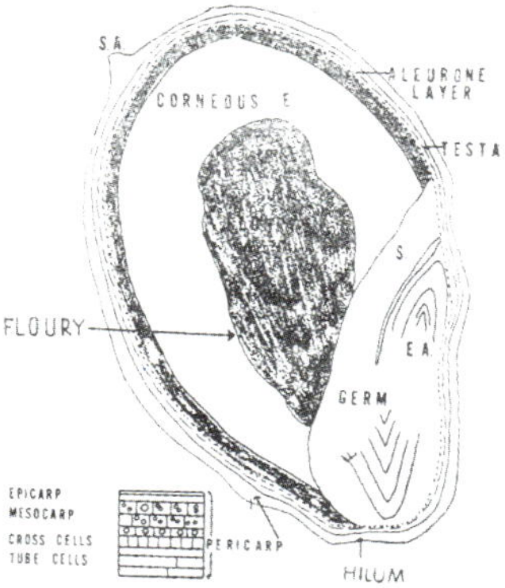

Plate No. 1. Sorghum grain structure

Plate No. 3. The stone mill and the pestle-mortar system used for milling cereals in India

1

2

3

Plate No. 2. Flourmills; 1. Vertical mill, 2. Horizontal mill and 3. Pin mill.

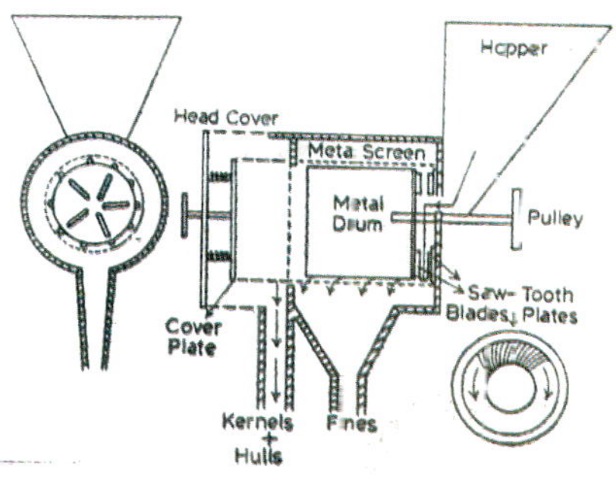

Plate No. 4. Schematic diagram of the attrition mill
Source: Reichert and Young, 1976

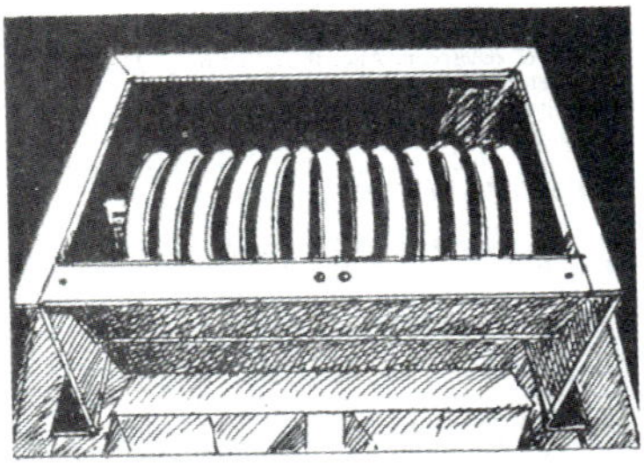

Plate No. 5. Dry milling of grain sorghum
Source: Reichert and Young, 1976

Plate No. 6. Dehulling/Pearling Machine

Sorghum Beer

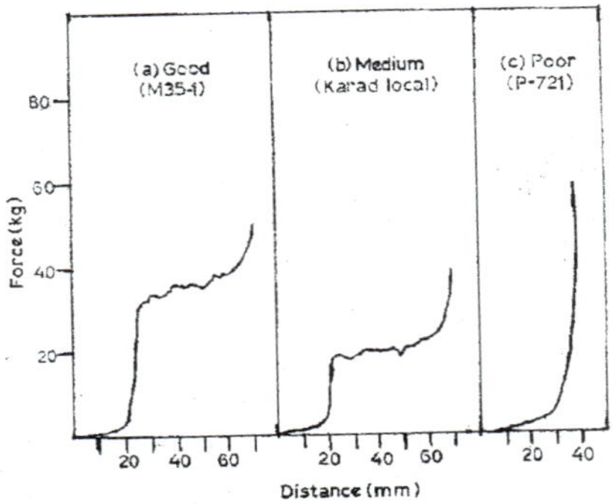

Plate No.7. Force-distance curves for good, medium and poor quality doughs of sorghum flour (Instron).

Plate No. 8. Matted Sorghum Grains

Plate No. 9. Sorghum Bread

Cooked grains

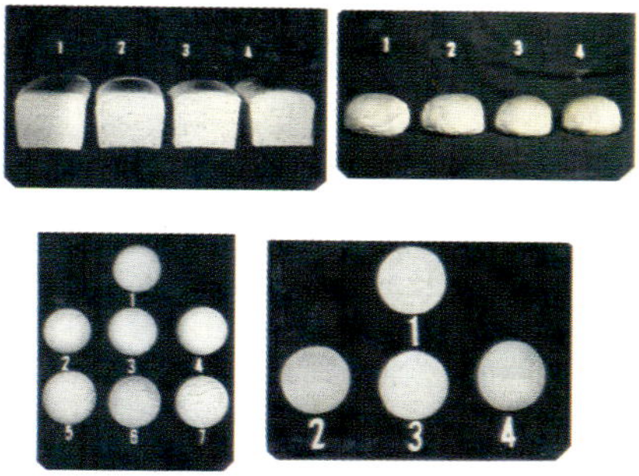

Plate No. 10. Bread, buns, cookies and biscuits prepared using sorghum flour.

Sorghum Pops

Pop laddu

Sorghum Hurda

Sorghum laddu

Pop grits chikki

Pop flour chikki

Raw flakes

Processed flakes

Fine flour

Semolina / Rava

Noodles

Noodles Kheer

Modak

High fiber Sorghum Papad

Malted Sorghum

Upama

Papad press machine

Pakoda

Normal Papad

Shira (sweets)

Idali

Idali

Dosa

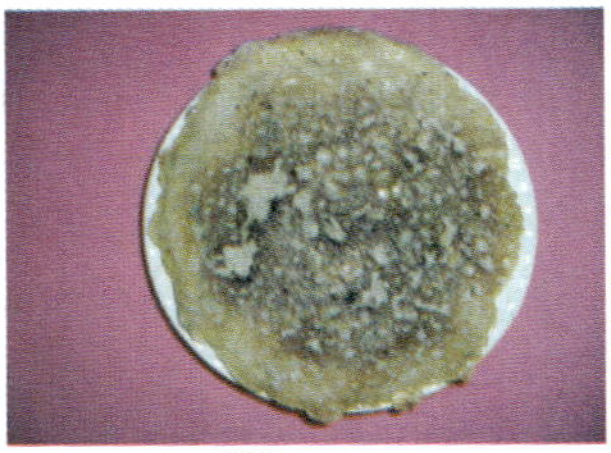

Uttappa

Rava laddu

Plane Chakali

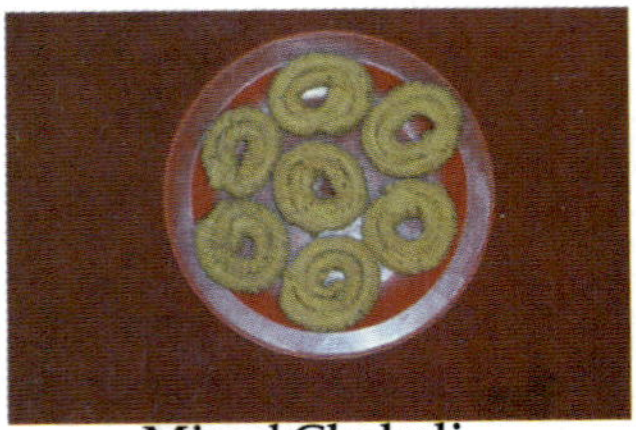

Mixed Chakali

Masala Chakali

Shev

Papadi

Papadi

Shnkarpale

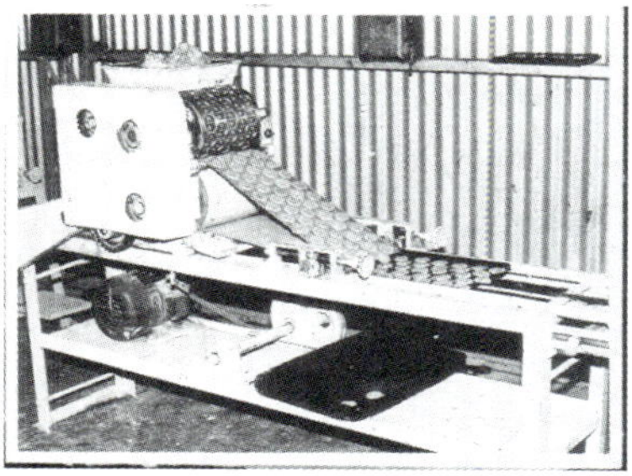

Biscuits making machine

Cake

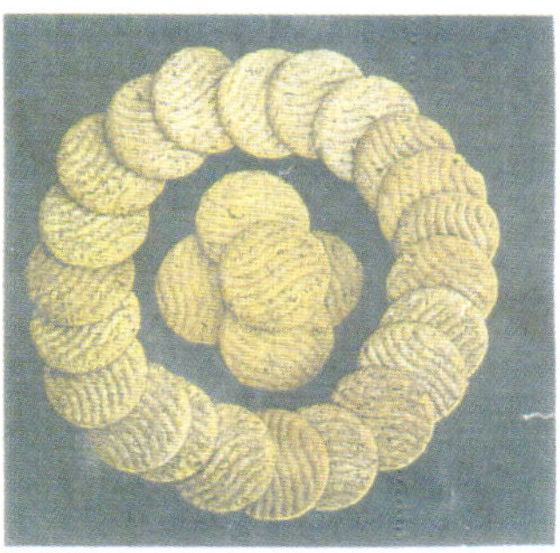

Biscuits

Sorghum Starch

Nankatai

Plate No. 12. Sorghum Syrup

Sorghum Product Cafe

Plate No. 13. Ethanol industry and storage containers